MW01286732

a
cursed
collection *of*
Haunted
Dolls

About the Author

Fiona Dodwell is a freelance writer and author. She has produced content for many companies, websites, and publications, including *Haunted Magazine, Made in Shoreditch Magazine,* Music-News.com, and many more. She loves writing and researching all things paranormal. In her spare time, she loves reading, attending investigations of haunted locations, and bingeing spooky podcasts. If you want to contact Fiona, or you want to share your own haunted doll story with her, you can reach her on her social media:

X: @Angel_Devil982
TikTok: @fiona_dodwell

a
cursed
collection *of*
Haunted
Dolls

FIONA DODWELL

LLEWELLYN
WOODBURY, MINNESOTA

FIRST EDITION
First Printing, 2025

Cover design by Kevin R. Brown
Interior illustrations by the Llewellyn Art Department
Peggy the Doll interview with Jayne Harris originally published: https://the hauntedattic.uk/2016/06/16/interview-with-jayne-harris-in-pursuit-of-the -paranormal/.
Harold the Doll interview with Anthony Quinata originally published: https:// thehauntedattic.uk/2015/10/18/harold-the-haunted-doll-an-infamous-case -of-the-paranormal/.
List of trademarked dolls on page 191.

Llewellyn Publications is a registered trademark of Llewellyn Worldwide Ltd.

Library of Congress Cataloging-in-Publication Data (Pending)
ISBN: 978-0-7387-8071-9

Llewellyn Worldwide Ltd. does not participate in, endorse, or have any authority or responsibility concerning private business transactions between our authors and the public.

All mail addressed to the author is forwarded but the publisher cannot, unless specifically instructed by the author, give out an address or phone number.

Any internet references contained in this work are current at publication time, but the publisher cannot guarantee that a specific location will continue to be maintained. Please refer to the publisher's website for links to authors' websites and other sources.

Llewellyn Publications
A Division of Llewellyn Worldwide Ltd.
2143 Wooddale Drive
Woodbury, MN 55125-2989
www.llewellyn.com

Printed in the United States of America

GPSR Representation:
UPI-2M PLUS d.o.o., Medulićeva 20, 10000 Zagreb, Croatia,
matt.parsons@upi2mbooks.hr

Other Books by Fiona Dodwell

Nails

The Hidden

Disclaimer

Given the nature of this topic, the author and publisher have opted to use illustrations of dolls in place of real photos. Please note that viewing photos of some haunted dolls may result in bad luck, feeling sick, or other adverse side effects. Be careful when doing research about and viewing photos of haunted dolls. The publisher and the author assume no liability for any injuries caused to the reader that may result from the reader's use of the content contained herein and recommend common sense when contemplating the practises described in the work.

Dedication

For my wonderful dad, Roger, who ignited in me a passion for the unusual from the earliest days.

Special thanks to my husband, Matthew, for his constant support and encouragement.

CONTENTS

Foreword by Fred Batt   xv

Introduction   1

Chapter 1: History of Dolls and How They
   Become Haunted   5

Chapter 2: Famous Cases   25

Chapter 3: Unknown and Lesser-Known Cases   37

Chapter 4: Edna and Bonnie   53

Chapter 5: Interviews with Owners of Haunted Dolls   69

Chapter 6: Dolls in Film   125

Chapter 7: Dolls in Literature   169

Conclusion   179

Acknowledgments   181

Bibliography   183

Doll Trademarks   191

FOREWORD

I am a demonologist, and I have studied all sides of the paranormal from about the age of fourteen. And now, according to many on the internet and worldwide, I am probably the most well-known demonologist there is. This is mainly due to my appearances on the hit TV show *Most Haunted* (which for the past twenty years has been shown in over ninety-four countries and was the first TV show to deal with the paranormal).

What is a demonologist? Basically, it is someone who studies demons, and when you think of demons, you are thinking of the most horrific and dangerous side of paranormal activity. You might then ask, What has this to do with dolls? It has an awful lot to do with dolls, and I don't just mean the ones in the Hollywood films. I have witnessed many disturbances caused by an out-of-control doll. They can be "taken over" or possessed by an evil spirit, better known as a demon. I was called to a house a couple of years ago in the North of England where there was a major disturbance going on in a child's bedroom. The child had told his mother that he had a friend in his bedroom that came to play every night. It was described by the child as a male with a burnt face, and to cut a long story short, I discovered the spirit child had been in a fire in the previous house that was on the land.

The reason I have mentioned this story is because of what happened in the child's bedroom when it was empty. The mother had reported to me that from downstairs she could hear someone in there, and she asked me to come and investigate. When I arrived, I could hear the noise for myself coming from upstairs: I could hear children's laughter and what sounded like whistles and mechanical noises. I slowly climbed the stairs not knowing what I would find, but it was a child's bedroom, so I expected it to be full of toys and nice things. The noise got louder as I reached the bedroom door. I slowly opened it just enough for me to see inside without whatever was in there seeing me! I was so shocked; it was like I had opened the door of an animated toy display at a department store at Christmas. There were toy cars driving round in circles, a toy fire engine driving round with its blue lights and horns going, and this giant teddy bear sitting in the corner, which, it seemed, had spotted me. Its head turned round and looked me straight in the eyes. I opened the door fully and everything stopped immediately. Then, I had the job of getting rid of what was there and getting some peace back in the place, which I did. And yes, it was demons—not just one but three. So, a few chants in Latin, and they were sent back to where they belong. So, it shows you that it doesn't only happen to dolls.

My first encounter with a doll was many years ago when I was involved with "showmen"—people who own and run fairgrounds. In those days, there were many strange side-shows at every fairground, and the most popular ones were the "freak shows." You would pay something like one pound to enter. One day, I entered a show, and sitting in there with chains fixed to it inside a heavy wooden case with a tough-ened glass front surrounded by more chains and padlocks was this very old, very ragged, and unkempt sad-looking doll.

I asked the owner of the show about the doll, and he told me a very strange but intriguing story. It had been in his fam-ily forever, and a story had been handed down through the generations of the doll known as Alice. The story goes that Alice was a real girl from a very noble family in the 1700s; she was the daughter of a lord and was known throughout the land as a stunningly beautiful girl. Many men were hop-ing they would win the hand of Alice in marriage, but her father was very protective, and, in his eyes, nobody was good enough to marry her. He even had a doll made of her, and the doll was just as beautiful. One day while travelling home in her carriage, she suddenly came to an abrupt halt. Three rogues stepped out from the darkness and dragged her from the carriage and carried her away on one of their horses, never to be seen again. The only thing left in the carriage was the doll. The lord offered a large reward and her hand in marriage for her return, but she was never found.

The owner of the sideshow said that he wanted to get rid of the doll because it was a well-known fact that it brought bad luck to so many people. I said I would be happy to take it off his hands. He said there is one very important condition that must be upheld: Money has to change hands to keep away the bad luck, and if you sell it on, you must also take money for it. If you do this, everything will be fine. The first thing I thought was that he was telling me an old travellers' tale to get money for it, but then, to my shock, he said, "Just one penny will do." So I was wrong; he wasn't trying to turn me over at all. I gave him the penny, and I have now owned the doll for about forty years. But one thing worries me: As I was walking away, he shouted out, "Make sure you keep her in chains."

Well, so far, so good!

The book in your hands is a detailed and informative look at the world of haunted dolls, and I know it was certainly a labour of love for the author. I think it's vital that we take a closer look at this type of phenomenon, as activity around haunted objects is increasing and not always easy for people to deal with. That's why books like this one are so important. They raise awareness as well as entertain us.

—Fred Batt, demonologist
The Fred Batt Appreciation Group (Facebook)

INTRODUCTION

I've been fascinated with ghosts and hauntings since I was a child. I can't really pinpoint the moment this interest gripped me because it's been there for as long as I can remember.

It started with reading books of short ghost stories as a kid and creating creepy tales to regale my friends with at sleepovers. Then as a teen came the obsession with scary movies and trips to creepy locations. I loved nothing more than a Sunday afternoon stroll around local graveyards. Over time, my interest became a part of me. Studying ghosts and hauntings was no longer just a hobby; it became a central part of who I am. It was then, and it still is today. It feels like a calling.

I began to seriously examine the paranormal as time went on. I studied demonology under Bishop James Long, undertook a diploma in applied paranormal research, enrolled in several courses under the guide of parapsychologist Dr. Ciarán O'Keeffe, and also studied theology. I attended many allegedly haunted locations and investigated them with others. It was my fascination which fuelled me, but more than that, my own supernatural experiences did, of which I have had a few.

One aspect of the paranormal that really intrigued me was the idea of objects being haunted—in particular, dolls. It may stem from the movies I grew up watching, such as *Child's Play* and *Dolly Dearest*. The idea that our innocent-looking toys could harbour something sinister or paranormal really gripped me. It was a concept that really drew me in, and I spent vast amounts of time researching cases of haunted dolls. There are, surprisingly, quite a lot of them.

After a while, I decided I needed to compile my thoughts, interviews, research and ideas into a book, which is what you are holding right now. I wanted to put together a project that discusses not only cases of haunted dolls but gains insight about them through conversations with paranormal experts and owners of spirited dolls. I speak with people who have experienced hauntings because of them, and for those who like a bit of creepy entertainment, I have also put together a guide to films and books that use haunted or cursed dolls as a catalyst. The impact of haunted dolls on entertainment culture simply cannot be ignored.

Why Dolls?

Often, people ask me why I am so drawn to this subject. There's just something about dolls, though, isn't there? They were designed to be the innocent play-friends of children across the world, yet over time, their image has transformed in the minds of many. From a cute and humble toy, they have slowly emerged as possessed, malevolent vessels that can bring death and destruction to those who unwittingly have one in their home.

It might seem quite a leap for some that those cute little dolls with the wide and innocent eyes can somehow be a harbinger of bad luck and possible death. How did we arrive at this point, where the once-cooed-over dollies of our childhood have come to represent something far darker and more sinister? That was the biggest question, the driving force that inspired me to write this book.

Popular culture seemed to be itching from the get-go to create something darker out of our cute playmates. Whether it's the evil ventriloquist doll of *The Great Gabbo* movie in 1929, or the mini ginger psycho killer of Chucky in Don Mancini's legendary Child's Play franchise, our films have long been depicting dolls as something to be feared rather than played with.

Perhaps it was the infamous story of the haunted doll Annabelle that firmly turned the tide of opinion against these toys. Although evil dolls were used in films going back as far as the 1920s, there was certainly a wider cultural shift in our perception of them after the story of the possessed doll Annabelle. She made headlines in the '70s after famed paranormal investigators and demonologists Ed and Lorraine Warren publicly spoke about the doll they claimed was inhabited by an inhuman spirit.

There were articles, books, and films over the years all about the Annabelle doll—that cute Raggedy Ann with the red yarn for hair. Maybe that was the turning point, the moment that people started to look twice at those seemingly innocent toys and began to ponder darker thoughts about them.

Contained in this volume are many years of research and study into the subject. I hope you enjoy reading the results of my work as much as I enjoyed producing it.

CHAPTER 1
HISTORY OF DOLLS AND HOW THEY BECOME HAUNTED

People have had a fascination with dolls since they first existed. Whether it be the earliest-known examples, such as those made from wood, clay, or stone, or the curious modern reborn dolls (baby dolls made to appear eerily lifelike), they have gripped us, arousing our curiosity and emotions.

Wooden paddle dolls are said to be amongst the earliest, having been found primarily in Egyptian tombs that date from 2000 BCE. Such early finds show us just how these little human replicas are deeply embedded in our collective history and culture. Although it is known that, historically, dolls were usually created for ritual purposes rather than for play, they clearly had a place in early societies. Whatever their purpose, history shows us that we are drawn to humanlike vessels. They call to us.

Primitive dolls known as *shabti* have been found in Egyptian burial tombs as early as 1985–1773 BCE.[1] These figures were created to represent the deceased. They were often made of simple materials, such as clay and wax. Even more astounding is the report of the discovery of a 4,500-year-old doll found in the grave of a Bronze Age child in Siberia.[2] Discoveries such as those remind us of how deeply ingrained our love of dolls is—children have long been seeking out human replicas to love, cuddle, and take care of.

It was in the fifteenth century that doll manufacturing became widespread. Germany took the lead in the production of these childhood favourites. The US followed suit in the early 1800s with the opening of the Tower Toy Company.

Through the years, we've seen them all, haven't we? From Barbies and Cabbage Patch Kids to collectible porcelain dolls. The list is endless. Not all dolls were intended as children's playthings, though. Throughout history, dolls have been used in religious rites, for entertainment, and even as teaching tools. Greek brides, for example, used to offer their dolls to the gods before getting married as a symbol of their journey from childhood to womanhood.

---

1. "What Is a Shabti?" National Trust, accessed March 4, 2025, https://www.nationaltrust.org.uk/discover/history/art-collections/shabti-faqs.

2. Roger Baird, "World's Oldest Toy Unearthed in Siberian Grave of Bronze Age Child Buried 4,500 Years Ago," International Business Times, December 29, 2017, https://www.ibtimes.co.uk/worlds-oldest-toy-unearthed-siberian-grave-bronze-age-child-buried-4500-years-ago-1653109.

Dolls with a Dark History

Let's take a look at some of the more macabre and notable dolls produced throughout history.

Voodoo Dolls

These are essentially effigies (something made in the image of someone or an item that represents someone). Throughout history, dolls like this have been used all over the world in various traditions and practises. Voodoo, also known as Vodou (accepted by many as the more respectful name), is a religion that can be traced back to Haiti. It is a religion still practised by many African Americans; however, the idea of the dolls being created to cause harm to an individual is not all it seems. Those who practise the religion use the dolls as a way to contact spirits for rituals and often for healing. The idea of the voodoo doll as a tool to bestow a curse is something that has been adopted by popular culture. However, dolls used to cause harm have very little place in the religion and are not used by the majority of practitioners. Throughout history, there *have* been times when dolls were used to cause harm. In ancient Egypt, for example, people sometimes used dolls to perform a curse and binding rituals.

The Voodoo pin or spell dolls you see in tourist areas of New Orleans and online are often sold as souvenirs and are not a reflection of the true history and purpose of the dolls.

Victorian Mourning Dolls

From the mid-nineteenth century right up to the early 1900s (which was a time of high death rates amongst both children and adults), mourning dolls were used by Victorians as decorations for the graves of deceased boys and girls. The dolls were commissioned by families in their child's honour. Commonly known as *grave dolls*, they would usually be made out of wax and would often be life size. The doll would be dressed using the dead child's clothes, and often, sections of hair from the deceased would be used as a wig for the doll. They were usually filled with sand to give them solid weight and would then be displayed during the funeral before being placed on the grave.

Dolls in the Modern World

It was in the sixteenth century that dolls went into full manufacturing. Throughout the seventeenth and eighteenth centuries, dolls were being crafted from a variety of materials including wood, wax, and papier-mâché. Dolls were usually created with china faces during the early nineteenth century, and until the late 1800s, the bodies were often made of fabrics and stuffed with sawdust and soft material. It wasn't until the 1940s that dolls were made with plastic or synthetic materials, such as with the much-loved walker, or Pedigree, dolls.

As time went on and dolls went into full production around the world using more child-friendly materials, brands such as

Barbie (1959) and Chatty Cathy (1960s) made appearances. They were huge hits amongst children.

Ventriloquism and Dummies

The art of ventriloquism made dolls popular in a very unique way. (*Ventriloquism* is the act of an artist directing their voice so it appears to be coming from a prop, doll, or dummy.) There is evidence of the practise as far back as 2000 BCE in Egypt and across the ancient world. It eventually gained momentum as an act at fairs and travelling shows. It was Fred Russell who performed ventriloquism in the modern sense by engaging with a dummy in conversation on stage in 1886. The act proved hugely successful and spawned a whole new generation of entertainers. It became especially popular in the 1960s.

The term *ventriloquism* derives from the Latin *ventriloquus*, "to speak from the stomach" (*venter* meaning "belly" and *loqui* meaning "speak"). At its inception, it was viewed as a practise of communicating with the dead. The voices and noises produced by a ventriloquist in this manner were said to be from the deceased, and it was up to the artist to "interpret" what the departed were trying to convey to the living.

By the mid-1800s, the supernatural aspect of ventriloquism subsided, and the act was rebranded as fun entertainment. It has had waves of popularity over the years, with the practise going in and out of style, but it is still a respected form of showmanship today.

Literary examples of frightening ventriloquist dummies include Gerald Kersh's *The Horrible Dummy and Other Stories* and the story "The Glass Eye" by John Keir Cross.

Frozen Charlottes

Frozen Charlottes are small china dolls that were made between 1850 and 1920, and they were extremely popular figurines in their time. It was only later that they became known as Frozen Charlottes, though, after they became associated with the poem by Seba Smith. (Some attribute the poem to his wife, Elizabeth Oakes Smith.) The poem was eerily called "A Corpse Going to a Ball."[3]

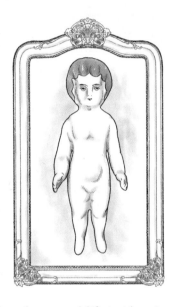

The poem was allegedly based on a real-life incident in which a young woman supposedly froze to death on her way to a New Year's Eve ball. As if the story isn't creepy enough, this piece focuses on the dying woman. The poem details the

---

3. Bonnie Taylor-Blake, "Defrosting Frozen Charlotte: 21st-Century Misconceptions about a 19th-Century Doll," *So They Say* (blog), WordPress, July 6, 2019, https://btaylorblake.com/2019/07/06/defrosting-frozen-charlotte-21st-century-misconceptions-about-a-19th-century-doll/.

journey of a young woman on a freezing-cold night travelling to a party. It is only as the horse and carriage pull up at the ball that those around her realise the girl is dead: She has frozen.

These tiny dolls were given to children, and it became tradition to place the Frozen Charlottes into Christmas cakes so that children having a slice of the delicious treat might be the lucky one to find the doll in their food.

You can still buy Frozen Charlottes today if you scour secondhand and antique stores, or eBay listings.

It is safe to say that dolls, in all their manner of production, presentation, and history, are fascinating. However, the reason for this book is to look at a very specific question: Is it truly possible for a doll to be haunted, and if so, how?

How Can Objects Become Haunted?

Whilst there is a wealth of articles, books, and videos detailing evidence of items such as dolls being haunted, the root issue of *how* these items have become spirited is not always so clear.

There are a few prevailing theories on why dolls, toys, and jewellery (amongst many other examples) might become haunted, and those are probably a good place to begin before we take a closer look at the case studies detailed in this book.

The Energy of a Previous Owner

An item such as a beloved children's doll or a much-treasured wedding ring can, over time, begin to mean a lot to the person who owns it. If the doll is carried around by a child who adores it and keeps it over the years, loving it, cuddling it, and even projecting a personality onto it (perhaps even keeping it on a shelf well into adulthood and old age), that item can potentially "absorb" some of the energy of the person who owns it.

Conduit

A *conduit*, in spiritual terms, refers to an item that can be used and manipulated by spirits to engage and communicate with someone. For example, a spirit may use a doll to draw in the attention of a person. A good example of this is Annabelle the Doll, in which it is alleged that a demonic entity used the doll as a conduit.

Cursed Items

Curses are very different from hauntings. A curse means that somebody has intentionally focused their energy or a spell onto an object so that it can bring about bad luck or damage to a person. For instance, a curse may be placed upon a doll and then given as a gift to a family. This is one of the theories that is alleged to have happened with the infamous Robert the Doll, of which you will read more about later. Essentially, the negative energy is coming from the doll, but it is not from a ghost or a previous owner's energy; it is from the curse itself that somebody has attached to it.

Spirit Attachment

Another theory is that some spirits, without having a physical body, are drawn to these humanlike vessels. It may not be that a soul is "trapped" within a doll (such as with horror films like *Child's Play*), but it is more likely that a spirit feels drawn or connected to something that is distinctly human-looking in appearance.

Psychic Imprint, or Stone Tape Theory

The stone tape theory is a popular one in paranormal circles, and it refers to the idea that houses and places exhibit paranormal reenactments due to highly emotional events. The spirits that appear may not be intelligent and able to communicate; instead, they are replaying a scene from the past, like a film playing on television. This idea can easily be applied to objects. For instance, an item that was close to a murder scene may soak up the energy of the event, and somebody who later owns the object may experience things associated with the highly charged past event.

Communicating with Haunted Dolls

You may have decided to buy an allegedly haunted doll, or you may believe an item in your possession is spirited, yet you are not psychic. What can you do to learn more?

If, like myself, you are fascinated by the paranormal and with spirit communication but you do not consider yourself psychic, it does not mean you are at a dead end, so to speak. There are many methods, experiments, pieces of equipment, and online tools you can use which can aid in personal research of a haunted object. Some of these you may have seen on organised "ghost hunts" or on paranormal television shows. Here are some items which have helped me so far in communicating with my own haunted doll, Edna. She will be discussed more in a later chapter. And they might be of value to you if you are an owner of a haunted doll or are hoping to adopt one.

EMF Meters

These devices light up when an unexplained energy source spikes near an area or object. They can range anywhere from £10 to £40 ($13 to $50). Simply place the device on the doll or item in question and ask the spirit to come close to it. The theory is that the energy will cause the lights to flash on the gadget.

Cat Balls

Cat balls are little plastic balls that light up and flash, but only when touched or moved. So, if one lights up when no one is near it or touching it, then it could indicate spirit presence has manipulated it.

Paranormal Apps
Opinions are hugely divided when it comes to apps. Many in the paranormal field have very little time for them, but there are a select few that are considered reliable and more trustworthy. It's worth taking your time to read reviews and articles in order to find the best ones available, or ones suited to your own preferences.

Dictaphone
This is one of my favourites. Over my years of paranormal investigations and ghost hunts, I have found that the most fascinating and validating piece of equipment is a basic audio recorder or Dictaphone. Recording yourself whilst asking questions out loud can allegedly result in capturing spirit voices in response, which for many helps to confirm the existence of spirits and their intelligent ability to communicate.

Pendulum
Many people are wary of Ouija boards, and perhaps understandably so, but another method of communication that appears to be more "safe" is a pendulum. You can buy these for very little cost, and the idea is to hold one gently in the air and ask a spirit to move the pendulum for yes-and-no responses.

It's cheap and easy, but many paranormal enthusiasts are very passionate about the results this item yields.

Why Do We Find Dolls So Unsettling?

Hauntings and ghosts aside, it's clear that there are many of us who find dolls creepy. Could this be the reason why we find the idea of them being haunted so easy to accept? I wanted to find out more about the psychology behind why we find dolls a little unnerving. Is there a good reason for this?

I reached out to Dr. Steph Lay, who is an Open University manager and psychology researcher in the UK. She has studied the psychology of why we find near-human things such as dolls so creepy and why we might think there's more to them than meets the eye.

Here, in her own words, Steph lays out for us why we find dolls so unsettling.

Back when I started my research into the phenomenon called the *uncanny valley*, it really came from my interest in all things strange, spooky, and disquieting. I was gifted a mascot to watch over the long hours I'd be spending at the computer, and this eerie Japanese doll, with her long black hair, blank face, and empty dark eyes, came to embody a lot of the questions I was looking to answer: Why do people find her so unsettling, and what is it about some faces which are almost but not quite human that [make] us feel so uneasy when other nonhuman faces are completely acceptable? The theory goes that it's all to do with them being nearly but not quite human. To start with, the more realistic a doll, statue, or robot becomes, the more we feel that we like it, right up to the point where it tips into being so humanlike that it becomes frightening, and at that moment, our liking for it turns into feelings of disquiet or even disgust.

But why? I noticed that, like with the doll above, these responses were particularly strong where there was something unusual about the eyes. I had a theory that this might be because eyes are usually so expressive and meaningful that anything unusual there would make it hard for us to guess what the other person was really thinking. To test this, I showed people pictures of faces and asked them to rate how humanlike, strange, and eerie they thought they were. The pictures had been digitally altered to mix up the expressions that they were showing. So, for example, a sad face could be shown with angry or frightened eyes. Over a large number of different combinations, the ones that were rated as the most eerie were those where a very happy face had angry or frightened eyes … I linked this to previous research that had found that the only times where we'd encounter this sort of face would be when someone is trying to hide a strongly felt emotion from us. Someone pretending to be happy when they're actually feeling angry or fearful is likely to want to cause us harm, so it would be sensible of us to try to avoid them!

My research used pictures of adult faces, but the fear that this type of mismatch causes can help us to understand why it's so easy for us to find dolls spooky and to believe that they might be haunted. Generally, dolls look like young humans, and childhood is traditionally seen as an innocent and hopefully happy time. However, even the most realistic doll will have blank, lifeless eyes. This strong mismatch between an impression of playful innocence combined with eyes you really can't read sets up a disquieting sense that there's something subtly wrong about what we are seeing. Once that unsettling feeling has set in, it can become all too easy to believe that there might be something even darker lurking within.

So, You Still Want to Buy a Haunted Doll

While many of us might actively avoid having a haunted item in our home, there are some who scour the internet and secondhand stores in search of dolls that are allegedly haunted or cursed. To some, the idea may be complete madness, but the growing industry of haunted doll sales on auction site eBay alone shows us there is a huge demand from people to have their own slice of the paranormal.

Of course, with horror films becoming huge cult classics, such as *Annabelle* and *Child's Play*, there was bound to be an interest in scary dolls amongst fans and the public in general, but few of us could have imagined the impact this haunted doll movement online would go on to have.

One of the first (and most famous) haunted items to ever be sold online was through eBay and was, in fact, not even a doll. It was known as a *dybbuk box* (a Jewish wooden box said to contain a demon). This item was sold on an eBay listing by Kevin Mannis in 2003, who wrote that the item had once been owned by a Holocaust survivor from Poland and that the box was home to an evil energy. Although Mannis allegedly recanted details from his own account, the box passed eventually to Jason Haxton, who wrote of his own experiences with it.[4] He eventually gave it to paranormal star Zak Bagans to exhibit in his Haunted Museum (where it still resides at the time of writing).[5] No, the *dybbuk box* isn't a doll, but it did give birth to a bigger trend of selling such items online—dolls proving to be the most popular items to be traded and sold.

One only has to open a web page and type in "haunted dolls" to be met with hundreds of listings of haunted dolls. One of the most popular of recent times was the haunted bridal doll, which became infamous after an appearance on UK daytime TV show *This Morning*. Collector Debbie Merrick purchased three dolls secondhand for just £5 each, only to realise the bridal doll was haunted. Merrick claimed that the doll caused her alarm to keep going off and was the perpetrator behind scratches that appeared on her partner. Merrick eventually sold the doll to the owner of a paranormal

4. Jessica Belasco, "Story of Haunted Box Isn't Just a Tale Dreamed Up in Hollywood," *San Antonio News*, updated September 21, 2012, https://www.mysanantonio.com/news/local/article/story-of-haunted-box-isn-t-just-a-tale-dreamed-up-3882396.php; Leslie Gornstein, "A Jinx in a Box?" *Los Angeles Times*, July 25, 2004, https://www.latimes.com/la-ca-urban-legend-jewish-scroll-cabinet-t-20040725-story.html; Charles Moss, "Finally, the Truth Behind the 'Haunted' Dybbuk Box Can Be Revealed," Inverse, July 8, 2021, https://www.inverse.com/input/features/dybbuk-box-dibbuk-kevin-mannis-zak-bagans-haunted-hoax-revealed.

5. Christopher Lawrence, "Zak Bagans Conquered the Dybbuk Box During His Quarantine," *Las Vegas Review-Journal*, June 5, 2020, https://www.reviewjournal.com/entertainment/tv/zak-bagans-conquered-the-dybbuk-box-during-his-quarantine-2045965/.

magazine for £866, showing just how much demand there is for an allegedly haunted item.[6]

Another famous doll that was purchased online was Harold the Doll. Harold was listed on eBay in 2003. The original seller claimed that the doll's presence and energy in their home caused the death of their cat, the end of their relationship, chronic migraines, and even disembodied voices in the basement. Harold was passed around from owner to owner before Anthony Quinata purchased him (see Harold's entry and Quinata's interview).[7]

One has only to search through the eBay app to see that hundreds, sometimes thousands, of allegedly haunted dolls are available for sale at any one time (667 at my current time of writing). Prices can range anywhere from as little as £3 to over £1,500.

At the time of writing, the most expensive haunted doll listed on eBay UK is from a seller who claims the large, black doll they are selling is inhabited by the spirit of Voodoo queen Marie Laveau. For £350, the very same seller listed a

---

6. This Morning, "My Haunted Doll Attacked My Husband | This Morning," YouTube, 5 min., 44 sec., July 24, 2017, https://www.youtube.com/watch ?v=f8nN-KG0UtM; Adam Miller, "This Morning Viewers Genuinely Terrified By Haunted Doll as They Spot THIS—Did You?" Express, July 24, 2017, https://www.express.co.uk/showbiz/tv-radio/832361/This-Morning -viewers-terrified-haunted-doll-rocking-chair-Ruth-Langsford-Eamonn -Holmes-ITV/1000.

7. Anthony Quinata, *Harold the Haunted Doll: The Terrifying, True Story of the World's Most Sinister Doll* (pub. by author, 2015).

porcelain doll said to be the vessel for an active spirit. Listings like this are just the tip of the paranormal iceberg.

Of course, it isn't just dolls. You can find pretty much any item with alleged spirit energy attached for sale online— from watches and teddies to jewellery and furniture. Dolls, though, seem to go that extra mile in getting attention. Maybe it's their lifelike eyes or the way in which horror films have roused our imaginations, letting us believe that maybe, just maybe, something alive exists behind those painted smiles…

How to Deal with a Haunted Item

If, after reading this book, you are convinced that an item in your possession is actually haunted, what is the best way to deal with it?

Keep It and Make Peace with It

You may be happy that the item is haunted; perhaps the attached energy is positive and a welcoming energy in your home and life. In that case, if there is no negativity or disturbance, you could possibly keep the item and carry on with life as normal. Keeping haunted items is considered a hobby by some, so you certainly aren't alone.

Binding and Other Rituals

Mediums, psychics, paranormal investigators, and certain priests, vicars, and reverends are able to bless an object to try to keep at bay any negatively charged energy associated with it. A binding ritual can also be performed, meaning that a spirit becomes tethered to an object and unable to freely cause havoc or paranormal disturbances.

If an item becomes too disturbing or causes demonic or highly negative events, a ritual can be performed and then the item can be removed from the home. There are individuals who keep objects like this locked safely away so others cannot come into direct contact with them. An example of this is the Raggedy Ann doll that inspired the Annabelle film franchise; this doll has resided for many years in the Warrens' Occult Museum behind glass, and no one is permitted to touch it.

CHAPTER 2
FAMOUS CASES

If you are somebody who has an interest in the paranormal and haunted objects, there's a significant chance you are familiar with a handful of the dolls I have selected to examine in this chapter of the book. It seems improper to ignore the more infamous cases such as Robert the Doll and Annabelle, so I have certainly included them due to their well-earned place in the history of haunted objects.

Here, you will meet the dolls who are famous the world over, and we will examine why.

Robert the Doll

This is perhaps one of the most famous cases of haunted dolls. Robert traces as far back as the early 1900s, when a young boy called Robert Eugene Otto was allegedly given the doll as a gift from a household maid. Over time, Otto began to believe the doll was haunted and claimed that Robert moved around, communicated with him, and caused all sorts of supernatural mischief in the family home. The doll wore an outfit that used to belong to Otto himself, a little sailor's suit.

In 1994, Robert was donated to the Fort East Martello Museum, where he went on display. At the time of writing, he is still there. Legend has it that if visitors take his photo without permission or disrespect him verbally they will suffer from bad luck.

The story of Robert the Doll has become infamous amongst those interested in the paranormal. Reports have circulated that those who take photos of Robert in his museum display without first asking the doll's permission end up cursed or experiencing bad luck. It may sound like something from a horror film, but apparently this phenomenon has affected people from all around the world.

Popular discussion site Reddit has a forum on the paranormal in which Robert has been discussed extensively. One user describes how their friend's sibling took a photograph of Robert and was plagued with bad luck. Not long after this, a picture they took in their own home appeared to have an apparition in it of a boy's face.[8]

On the website Tripadvisor, there are also tales of Robert bringing people bad luck. One user stated that since visiting Robert at the museum and taking his photograph, negative things have happened, including the breakdown of a relationship and losing a job.[9] They wanted to fix things, but how?

According to many, the only way to undo the bad luck or curse that follows a negative encounter with Robert is to apologise to him either to his face or by sending a letter to him at the museum. If this doesn't put you off, you can visit the doll at the museum and even do a ghost hunt there.

Annabelle

If you mention Annabelle the Doll to most people, chances are they will have heard of the demonic toy. Like most accounts that have had time to grow and evolve over time, however, the case of Annabelle has altered somewhat, with multiple different versions containing varying details coming to light. We'll get to the famous case soon, but first, here's some backstory.

---

8. SublimeSloth, "Friend Disrespected Robert the Doll in Key West. Cursed Photo Result Followed. 100% Real." Reddit, accessed March 4, 2025, https:// www.reddit.com/r/Paranormal/comments/15cjb97/friend_disrespected _robert_the_doll_in_key_west/?rdt=33995.

9. Michelle L., "Fun Little Side Tour," Tripadvisor, June 18, 2016, https://www .tripadvisor.co.uk/ShowUserReviews-g34345-d130356-r383757091-Fort _East_Martello_Museum-Key_West_Florida_Keys_Florida.html.

The Raggedy Ann doll was designed by Johnny Gruelle in 1915. His daughter, Marcella, allegedly found an old rag doll amongst several items in the attic, and Gruelle drew a face on the doll and gave it the name Raggedy Ann. Marcella was said to have loved the doll so much that her dad thought other children might go crazy for one, and so it was in 1915 that he created a patent for the doll.[10]

In a very upsetting turn of events, Marcella contracted diphtheria and died when she was thirteen. The devastating loss would surely have been a heavy blow to Gruelle, and perhaps the Raggedy Ann doll would forever remind him of his loss. The versions of this account vary, but the basic story remains. It is, without doubt, a sad story and one that would taint the doll's history.

Now, let's turn to the famous account, the one that has fuelled books, articles, and numerous horror films: the Annabelle case made known by Ed and Lorraine Warren, the demonologists who rose to fame in the '70s.

It was in 1970 when Donna, a nurse in her mid-twenties, was given a large Raggedy Ann doll from her mother, who was said to have seen it in a shop and thought it was the ideal present for her daughter. It was certainly an unusual and peculiar gift. Donna, however, had not owned the doll for too long before

10. Sally Lodge, "Raggedy Ann Turns 100," Publishers Weekly, PWxyz, September 22, 2015, https://www.publishersweekly.com/pw/by-topic/childrens/childrens-book-news/article/68132-at-100-raggedy-ann-embodies-a-creative-family-legacy.html.

she and her flatmate began to experience odd and inexplicable things in their shared home. For instance, there were times when the doll was left in one place in the flat, and upon Donna's return, the Raggedy Ann would be found in an entirely different location. There were notes too, allegedly scribbled in the writing of a child's hand, which were found beside the doll. These

events soon unnerved the young women, and they began to make a connection to the doll that Donna owned. They became convinced the Raggedy Ann was to blame for the creepy occurrences; they just didn't know how or why.

After some time of putting up with these upsetting events, it was decided that they needed help of some kind. A medium was called in to see what she could pick up on, and they were told that the doll was haunted by a child named Annabelle Higgins, aged seven. This child, they were informed, had passed away in their local area and wanted to possess the doll.

Thinking that a child would not possibly cause any harm, Donna is said to have permitted the ghost of the child to stay inside the Raggedy Ann. As much as she wished this was an end to the unsettling things that had been happening, events soon took a turn for the worse. There were marks found on the doll that looked like spots of blood. Around this time it is alleged that a friend of Donna's roommate began experiencing awful nightmares about the Raggedy Ann and was physically attacked with scratches appearing on their skin.

Donna and her friend eventually reached out to paranormal researchers and demonologists Ed and Lorraine Warren after being put into contact with them by a priest. The Warrens visited, willing to help, and took a close look at the doll. They soon confirmed there was indeed an energy linked to it, but it was not the spirit of a child. It was a demonic being who was trying to possess one of the women.

Donna wanted nothing more to do with the Raggedy Ann and asked the Warrens to take the doll away with them when they left. The item stayed with the Warrens, and they displayed it at their Occult Museum, where it was labelled with the now-famous warning: "Positively Do Not Open."[11]

As we have seen, Raggedy Ann dolls have been linked to dark occurrences, and it is easy to see why the history and the events surrounding them have gripped people the world over.

---

11. Katie Serena, "Meet the Real Haunted Doll Behind 'Annabelle,'" All That's Interesting, updated February 12, 2025, https://allthatsinteresting.com /annabelle-doll.

Peggy the Doll

One of the most well-known dolls to surface in recent years is Peggy, who made headlines in 2015. The doll allegedly caused heart attacks and upset in several people who had viewed her.

Jayne Harris, paranormal investigator and host of the TV show *Help! My House Is Haunted*, took the doll from a Sheffield garden shed. The doll had been left out there after the owner became uncomfortable with events that had begun unfolding in her home after taking the doll in. The woman had owned it for just a short time before finding herself experiencing the unsettling events in her home. She eventually decided enough was enough and took the doll to her shed, where it was left until Jayne came to help and remove it.[12]

I have interviewed and spoken with Jayne Harris several times and have completed a diploma in applied paranormal research under her guidance. I reached out to her to discuss

12. Louise Jew, "Stourbridge Mum Jayne Harris Reveals How She Became a Haunted Doll Investigator," Stourbridge News, September 4, 2015, https://www.stourbridgenews.co.uk/news/13646401.stourbridge-mum-jayne-harris-reveals-how-she-became-a-haunted-doll-investigator/.

Peggy and her experiences of studying the paranormal. It's safe to say, when it comes to haunted dolls, there are few people out there who know more about them than Jayne Harris. Jayne's experience in studying, investigating, and dealing with potentially haunted objects goes back a number of years. Even as a teenager, she felt her calling to become involved in the paranormal world.

> I started investigating alleged hauntings when I was fifteen, but purely as a hobby obviously. My parents used to visit Spiritualist churches, and I occasionally went along to see various speakers and mediums, and so this idea of survival post-death was just one I accepted growing up. As I got older, however, I began to hear other points of view and more psychological theories for what might be occurring, and so when I was around eighteen, I started employing a more diagnostic, scientific approach to claims of paranormal activity.

Jayne's passion soon turned to something more than just an interest and hobby.

> It wasn't until I joined social media that I discovered a wider community of like-minded people. And that's when my interest really started to become a

career. Today, I do all sorts of things from lecturing at schools and universities to TV work and writing.

Jayne spent a great deal of time undertaking the study of haunted dolls, but it was Peggy that really had a significant impact on not only Jayne's life but also on the wider paranormal community. She made an appearance on Zak Bagans's show *Deadly Possessions*, in which she took Peggy to meet Zak and discuss the doll's case in depth.

Yes, that was in December 2016, I think! My husband, Simon, and I were flown to Vegas (Peggy the Doll was sent separately), and we spent four days at his museum filming and investigating. The filming ended with a séance with psychic Patti Negri, and it was a most unusual experience, and things definitely happened in that room that were unexpected.

I asked Jayne to expand on her thoughts about Peggy.

Peggy the Doll was probably my most puzzling case. For whatever reason, people definitely *do* experience unusual things around that doll, and in extreme cases, we had reports of heart attacks and strokes. People who have visited the museum have reported a lot of things, and Zak was actually concerned at one point about people's safety and the risk Peggy might pose to the museum itself if he had to close. We came up with the idea of people signing waivers before they see her, so it really is all down to your own risk if you decide to go into her room.

With the tidal wave of items that are said to be haunted, and with more and more people coming forward to say they own spirited items, how does Jayne think it's best to verify if something is actually haunted? I was curious to know her thoughts.

I always start by trying to establish *why* people think the activity they are experiencing is the result of a specific object. Often, people may have inherited something from a deceased relative, for example, and because they have then subsequently been having dreams of that person or felt them around the home, they decide that it must be as a result of the object. A lot of the time, it's simply a psychological thing, triggered by the introduction of something which once belonged to that person.

And what about items that were not owned by a deceased relative, then? There's not such a level of emotional baggage, is there?

True. In cases where people have no idea about an object's history (maybe they bought it recently), then it becomes more interesting. In these cases, you really need to be looking at the potential haunting in the same way you would a potentially haunted building. If someone feels they [have] acquired a haunted object, they should set out monitoring and trying to record anything which they perceive as paranormal activity. [Keep] a log or diary of events, times, duration—that kind of thing—to see if any patterns emerge. It can be a long process and requires patience.

Verifying whether an item is haunted is not always easy, I imagine. Many people have personal experiences with a doll or object in their possession, but this may not be enough to incite belief amongst the more sceptical of us. Could science one day have the answers?

I think science can give us an insight into what may potentially await us after physical death. Trials have been set up whereby patients in ICU units have been monitored, and those who have been brought back to life as a result of resuscitation have reported having experiences when they have been clinically dead. Science can help us understand this if we give it enough of our time and attention. There are some things, however, which science cannot explain, as science is very restrictive in terms of its frameworks. Science is limited, for example.

I ask Jayne what she means by this, as so often people use the word *science* to deter people from believing in their own experiences.

> Science can explain to us the effects of the emotion love (things like raised heart rate, pupil dilation, lack of concentration, loss of appetite, and so on), but it cannot explain love itself. Emotions do not fit within a materialist framework, as they are not material, but that doesn't make them any less real. Likewise with consciousness. Brain scans can tell us which parts of the brain are active when we think, but they can't show where our thoughts come from, only that our brain is active at the time. It may well be that our brain is a receiver! So really, science has its limits, and what it is up to us to work out is how we can best use the limitations of science to further our knowledge and understanding.

With Jayne's impressive level of experience in and passion for the subject, it's easy to feel the infinite possibility that the study of the paranormal has. It feels, almost, as if we are still at the beginning and that we have so much more to learn.

CHAPTER 3
UNKNOWN AND LESSER-KNOWN CASES

The previous chapter explored cases of haunted dolls that you've probably at least heard of before, and they certainly have their reasons for being so infamous. In this chapter, though, I have taken a jump down the rabbit hole, uncovering accounts of haunted dolls that aren't as well known. Here, you may come across stories that you are not familiar with, which would be surprising, considering just how creepy they truly are.

Mandy

Currently residing in the Quesnel Museum in British Columbia, Mandy the Doll has made a name for herself as quite the spooky toy. Handed over to the museum back in 1991, the doll had originally belonged to the donor's grandmother. It had been left locked in a trunk for many years before finally finding a home on display. Mandy the Doll was given to the museum because she was fragile and gave the current owner a "weird feeling."[13]

Since the museum took the doll in and put her on display, there have been reports of creepy incidents. Some have said her eyes seem to follow you around, and with the amount of unease she caused to staff and visitors, Mandy was eventually placed in a secure glass cabinet. The doll was originally created in the early 1900s, making her a valuable collector's toy.

Staff members arrived at the museum one morning and found the lab had been left in a mess with no obvious explanation as to how it could have happened. And at another point, Mandy managed to leave her stuffed lamb on the floor despite being in a locked case.

Mandy has become a bit of a haunted doll celebrity, and has been featured in newspapers, on the radio, and on television. It was in 1999 that the doll met psychic Silvia Brown on *The Montel Williams Show*. The psychic, after spending time with the doll, came to believe it used to belong to twins who had died at an early age from polio.

Okiku

Okiku, who is also sometimes known as the Haunted Doll of Hokkaido, is a creepy-looking doll who currently sits in a temple in Iwamizawa. The legend goes that the doll is

---

13. "Mandy," Quesnel Museum & Archives, accessed January 27, 2025, https://www.quesnelmuseum.ca/node/264.

haunted by the ghost of a little girl—the girl who owned the doll before she died in 1918. According to one version of the legend, the girl loved the doll and often played with it. After she passed away from a severe cold, things started to go bump in the night in the family's home.

As the doll once belonged to the deceased child, the family didn't want to throw it away, and they kept it in their home family shrine for remembrance. They often spoke to the doll and prayed in front of it. At some point—and this is where things get really strange—the family began to notice that the doll's hair seemed like it was growing longer. The family decided this was a sign that their daughter was haunting the doll, and so the legend began. At some point, the family left the haunted doll in the care of monks at the Mannenji Temple in Iwamizawa. Monks there attested to the growing hair on the doll, and at one point even began regularly trimming it. The doll still stands at the site now. The hair is extremely long.

According to *Uncanny Japan*, a popular podcast, there are several different theories, stories, and misconceptions about the doll, all of which are explored in depth on their site.[14]

---

14. "Okiku: The Haunted Doll (Ep. 133)," Uncanny Japan, September 30, 2023, https://uncannyjapan.com/podcast/okiku-the-haunted-doll/.

Harold

When I think of haunted dolls, I think of my online friend and author Anthony Quinata. It was many years ago when I first came into contact with Anthony because I'd read his book on Harold, a doll he owned that was plagued with paranormal activity and bad luck. Anthony had purchased Harold on an online auction site and spent many subsequent years studying him and exploring his history and the many possible explanations for the phenomena surrounding the doll.

Anthony purchased Harold back in 2015. The doll was sold to him as a haunted object, and Anthony soon found himself facing all manner of paranormal and unexplained activity. The doll itself is a composition doll, likely made in the 1930s, and isn't in great shape at all. Anthony put his experiences in a book, *Harold the Haunted Doll*, and I soon found myself fascinated by the case.

The doll itself once appeared on the ghost-hunting series *Ghost Adventures* ("Island of the Dolls" episode). Since that time, people across the world have become fascinated by Harold and have been following his journey with Anthony.

Anthony himself became interested in ghosts and all things supernatural at the age of seven. His book *Communications from the Other Side: Death Is Not the End of Life, Love, or Relationships* discusses in depth how his journey into studying the paranormal developed.

According to previous conversations with Anthony, he had never actually intended to buy a haunted doll or a haunted object of any kind, but coming across Harold the Doll on an eBay listing soon changed that. And the rest, as they say, is history.

Anthony hesitated to label Harold as cursed or haunted. He also didn't believe that it was a case of possession. As far as he was concerned, whatever was going on was more severe than any of those three options.

Well, whatever the doll is, or whatever paranormal phenomena are associated with him, a whole host of scary and negative things happened in Anthony's life after taking the doll into his home.[15]

According to Anthony, the doll's negative energy was responsible for the death of his dog, Chance, and that loss, understandably, affected him deeply.

He also got messages from people describing how they experienced unexplained things just by reading a blog post

---

15. "Harold the Haunted Doll—An Infamous Case of the Paranormal," The Haunted Attic, accessed April 15, 2025, https://thehauntedattic.uk/2015/10/18/harold-the-haunted-doll-an-infamous-case-of-the-paranormal/.

about, seeing a video of, or looking at Harold. One message came from two men who saw Harold on the *Ghost Adventures* "Island of the Dolls" episode, mocked him, and then had to go to the emergency room.[16]

It seems Harold has a strong energy and one not to be messed with. Hearing Harold's story and the impact he has had on Anthony has been eye-opening to say the least. It makes this journey into the study of haunted dolls feel suddenly quite uncomfortable.

"The Hands Resist Him" Painting

Painted by artist Bill Stoneham in 1972, "The Hands Resist Him" is a painting which seems to unnerve a lot of people. It's easy to see why. I'm not sure if it's the girl doll (who has come to life) on the left-hand side or the disembodied hands clawing at the darkened window, but there is just something off about this depiction.

Allegedly, the boy in the painting is based on a photograph of the artist himself as a child. It is said that the doorway in the image symbolises the divide between our waking and dream worlds, while the doll is a kind of guide that helps the boy on his journey through those realms.[17] One family who purchased this painting said that the children's figures

---

16. "Harold the Haunted Doll."
17. "The Story of the eBay Haunted Painting, from the Artist's Perspective," Stoneham Studios, accessed February 19, 2025, https://stonehamstudios .com/haunted.

moved and that they had even caught this movement on camera. The family sold this painting on eBay, declaring that it was haunted. The eBay listing was viewed thousands of times. Some of these viewers complained to the seller about experiencing paranormal phenomena after merely visiting the listing.[18]

Rumours of previous owners dying and people hearing disembodied voices whilst viewing it have become legendary.

At the time of writing, the painting is kept at a gallery in Grand Rapids, Michigan.

The Island of the Dolls

If one haunted doll isn't quite enough for you, then maybe a holiday to Mexico might be in order. There, you will find La Isla de las Muñecas, otherwise known as the Island of the Dolls. Situated in Xochimilco (south of the centre of Mexico City), this spooky little island is inhabited by thousands of dolls. Some of them are in good condition; others are missing limbs or eyes. Most of them hang from the branches of trees, making them look like the victims of suicide.

The legend associated with the island goes back to a young girl who allegedly drowned in the nearby water. Forever roaming the earth, the child was said to remain on the island.

---

18. Jim Kershner, "Painting Goes Bump in the Night," The Spokesman-Review .com, October 31, 2002, https://web.archive.org/web/20050120212242 /http://www.spokesmanreview.com/news-story.asp?date=103102&ID =s1244540.

The man who discovered the girl's body was said to have found a doll floating in the water sometime later. The man, Don Julian Santana Barrera, said he believed the girl inhabited the doll, and he hung the doll from a tree to appease her spirit. Over time, he added more and more dolls to keep the spirit at peace. Now, it has become a hot spot for travellers interested in the weird and wonderful.

The Mannequin Corpse

This one might not come under the category of "doll," but it's certainly worthy of inclusion in this collection. Instead of a doll, this account focuses on a creepy-looking mannequin that sits in the display window of a Mexican bridal store. This mannequin has been the star of the shop since it was placed there in the 1930s.[19]

Legend has it that the store's owner at the time—Pascuala Esparza—was mourning

---

19. Lauren David, "La Pascualita: Bridal Shop Mannequin or Embalmed Corpse?" How Stuff Works, updated May 17, 2024, https://people.howstuffworks.com /la-pascualita.htm.

the loss of her daughter, who tragically died after allegedly being bitten by a black widow spider.

Over time, people began speculating that the very creepy and extremely lifelike mannequin was, in fact, the well-preserved corpse of the dead young woman. It's easy to see why: Most mannequins are not detailed at all but rather smooth and lacking in detail. This mannequin, however, has a very realistic-looking face and detailed skin, even down to the lines on the palms of her hands. Could this display item be, in fact, the dead woman herself?

Ruby

Currently one of the star attractions of the Traveling Museum of the Paranormal and the Occult, Ruby the Doll is known for making people feel sick and sad when they come into contact with her. Her story traces back many years to her original owners, one of whom allegedly died whilst clutching the doll. Soon after this death, spooky happenings started, and the family became convinced that the doll was haunted.[20]

---

20. Caitlin Busch, "'If They Don't Let Us Play, They All Go Away': Haunted Dolls That Would Scare Even Chucky," USA, August 23, 2022, https://www .usanetwork.com/usa-insider/scary-haunted-dolls-chucky; Maggie Miller, "Paranormal Playthings: The World's Most Famous Haunted Dolls," Travel Channel, accessed February 19, 2025, https://www.travelchannel.com /ghostober/articles/paranormal-playthings-the-worlds-most-famous -haunted-dolls.

Over the years, the family claimed that the doll would be found in different places and would move by itself.[21] You can visit her today at the Traveling Museum.

Charley

Charley was found in the attic of a Victorian house in 1968. The doll itself had been locked inside a trunk amongst old newspapers and a piece of paper upon which the Lord's Prayer had been written. The family who found him were apparently collectors of dolls and figurines, so rather than dispose of the doll or sell it, they decided to put it on display amongst their other collectibles. After a while, the family became convinced the doll was haunted because it moved on its own and was found in different places than where it had been left.

One of the young girls in the family started to tell stories about the doll talking to her and even blamed the doll for marks and scratches that appeared on her skin. So, the family locked Charley away again, despite initially suspecting it was the children doing such things. They could not ignore the fear that the presence of the doll ignited in the children. Over the years, the doll has changed hands several times amongst collectors; however, at the time of writing, Charley the Doll is on display at Local Artisan, an oddities and collectors shop in Massachusetts.

---

21. Busch, "'If They Don't Let Us Play.'"

The doll itself is possibly from the 1930s (although some believe it to be much older), as other items discovered in the old trunk in the attic were dated to around that era.[22]

Letta Me Out

Letta (also known as Letta Me Out) is a child-size doll who often creeps out whoever claps eyes on it. Said to be two hundred years old, Letta is made of wood, and apparently his wig is real human hair. The doll was said to have been discovered in an abandoned house by an individual named Kerry Walton, who was exploring the long-vacant property.[23] As all spooky stories go, once Walton took the doll back to his house, strange things began to happen. Items in the house began to move mysteriously, marks appeared on

---

22. Cynthia Auer, "Charley the Haunted Doll," Atlas Obscura, September 17, 2018, https://www.atlasobscura.com/places/charley-the-haunted-doll.

23. Lucia, "Encyclopaedia of the Impossible: Letta the Haunted Doll ('Letta Me Out')," The Ghost In My Machine, September 9, 2024, https://theghostinmy machine.com/2024/09/09/encyclopaedia-of-the-impossible-letta-the -haunted-doll-letta-me-out/; Meghan Harris, "Mystery Surrounds 200 -Year-Old 'Haunted Doll from Hell,'" The Courier Mail, October 11, 2016, https://www.couriermail.com.au/news/mystery-surrounds-200yearold -haunted-doll-from-hell/news-story/cdad1e331f15302212100f930d76f028.

surfaces, and animals would behave strangely around it.[24] One account stated that on one occasion, Walton tried to sell the doll, but when he attempted to get out of his car, he could not move, as if the doll was stopping him. He decided to keep the doll and now travels to different areas, allowing people to visit the spooky item. [25]

Joliet

Joliet is rumoured to be haunted, or, in some people's opinions, possessed. The legend associated with this antique doll is rather unsettling, to say the least. The story of Joliet is that the doll was passed on as a gift to several expectant mothers over the years, and on each occasion, the mother would have both a girl and a boy, only for the boy to die three days later.

Rumour had it that the doll was evil and would take the souls of the male children who died. Apparently, each person who owned the doll would then treat the doll like their own child, believing that the soul of their little boy was trapped inside the toy.

Anna, a member of the family who initially owned the doll, said that Joliet would make giggling sounds and that household pets were too nervous to be near the doll. The

24. "Meet One of Australia's Most Haunted Dolls in Warwick," *The Courier Mail*, March 1, 2018, https://www.couriermail.com.au/news/queensland/warwick /meet-one-of-australias-most-haunted-dolls-in-warwick/news-story /b787c3e75263b4f84ce03b19212ec45e.

25. Harris, "Mystery Surrounds 200-Year-Old 'Haunted Doll from Hell.'"

doll itself was said to have been given as a gift to a pregnant woman by a very jealous friend, who instigated the curse onto childbearing women.[26]

The Janesville Doll

A doll known as the Janesville Doll has been sitting in the attic of a home in Janesville, Minnesota, since the mid '70s. He sits by the attic window looking over the town, and his appearance there has prompted the imaginations of locals to run amok. His story is now a legend.

One version involves a tragic accident that took the life of a small child. The owner's daughter died, and the doll was placed in memorial for the lost soul.[27] Another version surrounds a single mother and her young child in a fight against evil. Reportedly, the woman's daughter became possessed by a demon, and she lost her life during an exorcism.[28] Scarier than that is the theory that the doll is actually a demon who watches over people in the local town in which it resides.[29]

Allegedly, the doll originally belonged to a man named Ward Wendt. He was born in the house, and he lived there

26. Ashley Hall, "Joliet—The Doll with a Haunting Curse," The Paranormal Guide, February 14, 2013, http://www.theparanormalguide.com/blog /joliet-the-doll-with-a-haunting-curse.

27. Dan Kettler, "The Janesville Baby," YouTube, 9 min., 34 sec., November 30, 2008, https://www.youtube.com/watch?v=lPxHLY1XAJo.

28. Orrin Grey, "What's That in the Window? The Creepy Legend of the Janesville Doll," The Lineup, June 28, 2016, https://the-line-up.com/janesville-doll.

29. Kettler, "The Janesville Baby."

until the day he died in 2012. Wendt placed the doll in the window, but he never told anyone why. He claimed he wrote the answer to the doll's existence in a note, which he placed in a town time capsule. Unfortunately, the capsule won't be opened until 2176, so the town will have to go a number of decades before the truth is finally revealed.[30]

Pupa

Pupa the haunted doll was created in the early 1900s, with a soft body and a wig of possibly human hair. She stands fourteen inches tall. According to the website The Ghost In My Machine, the doll was crafted by someone to look like the child it was being made for.[31] The doll was allegedly given to a young girl in Italy in the 1920s.

According to the story, the little girl who owned the doll said it was alive and would move around and talk to her. The girl kept hold of the doll well into adulthood until she

---

30. shawnfury, "Janesville, the Old Man & the Doll in the Window," TVFURY, October 3, 2012, https://tvfury.wordpress.com/2012/10/03/janesville-the -old-man-the-doll-in-the-window/; Clay Schuldt, "'World Has Always Been Crazy': Bizarre History Enthralls Audience," The Journal, January 22, 2021, https://www.nujournal.com/news/local-news/2021/01/22/world-has -always-been-crazy-bizarre-history-enthralls-audience.

31. Lucia, "Encyclopaedia of the Impossible: Pupa the Haunted Doll," The Ghost In My Machine, July 10, 2023, https://theghostinmymachine.com/2023 /07/10/encyclopaedia-of-the-impossible-pupa-the-haunted-doll/; Terri Lynn Vignes, "Haunted Doll," accessed January 28, 2025, https://web.archive.org /web/20070410112535/http://www.hauntedamericatours.com:80/haunted furniture/haunteddoll/myhaunteddoll/.

allegedly died in 2005. The owners who had the doll actually claimed it moved by itself; although she was encased in a clear display unit, they occasionally found her having moved inside it, appearing in different positions than how she had been left. Apparently, nobody knows where the doll currently resides today.

Haunted Bridal Doll

It was in 2017 that the infamous Haunted Bridal Doll made headlines. Then-owner Debbie Merrick spoke on UK TV show *This Morning*, claiming that the doll was haunted and that she had been experiencing paranormal occurrences in her home after buying the secondhand doll. She soon sold the bridal doll to paranormal investigator Lee Steer, who parted with £866 to buy her. Steer  did several investigations of the doll and publicly claimed that the spirit attached to it was responsible for physically attacking his father.[32] Steer named the doll Elizabeth and claimed to have caught paranormal phenomena on tape, which can be viewed on the video site YouTube.

Bebe

Bebe the Doll, who was produced in the 1970s, is owned by Janice, a collector of dolls. Janice was convinced that Bebe was haunted after several unusual and creepy occurrences happened in her home after purchasing her.

In her home, Janice heard unexplained noises and doors opening and closing. She once felt that she was being watched by something unseen in the house. Janice allegedly got her house blessed after events became unsettling for her, though things didn't settle afterward, unfortunately. Strange paranormal occurrences continued, and Janice found herself having a vision of an angry man.[33]

At the time of writing, little is known about Janice and whether Bebe's haunting energy continues, but it's a story that unsettles even the most hardened amongst us.

32. "'Possessed' China Doll Strikes Again! Mother Sells It for £1,000 on eBay After It 'Scratched' Her Husband—Only for New Owner to Claim His Father Has Now Been Attacked Too," *Daily Mail*, August 4, 2017, https://www .dailymail.co.uk/news/article-4760570/A-haunted-doll-flogged-eBay -attacked-new-owner.html.
33. ghostrekk, "Top 5 Most Haunted Dolls!!" Ghostrekk, February 17, 2016, https://ghostrekk.wordpress.com/2016/02/17/top-5-most-haunted-dolls/.

CHAPTER 4
EDNA AND BONNIE

In this chapter, we'll be covering two haunted dolls that I have had personal experiences with. I couldn't undertake the journey of putting this book together without opening myself up to experiencing haunted dolls myself, so that's exactly what I did. The results, as you will soon see, were eye opening.

Edna

Edna is a beautifully detailed porcelain doll that came into my life after a paranormal podcast episode was recorded about her. With creepy events that occurred during the recording of what would become a two-part special, I began communicating with the host, Rob Kirkup. He

soon opened up and shared his experiences with me, and it wasn't too long before Edna ended up in my own home and making her presence felt.

Rob runs the *How Haunted? Podcast* (how-haunted.com). Born in the northeast of England, he is an author, paranormal historian, and ghost hunter with over twenty years' experience.

Rob did a two-part special on his podcast about haunted dolls, and as a result, decided to spend two nights in a hotel room, just him and a doll called Edna. The results were surprising. There did, indeed, appear to be some kind of energy attached to the toy he had purchased online for the experiment.

> While working on episodes sixty-nine and seventy [of the podcast], a two-part special on haunted dolls, I had an idea. What if I bought a haunted doll of my own and spent some time with no one but the doll for company? It seemed like a good idea. No, a great idea. So, I opened up the eBay app and searched "haunted doll." There [were] loads of them. I looked through the photos, and there were dolls of all types—big ones, small ones, old ones, modern ones. There was even a haunted Smurf. The prices were as wide ranging as the dolls were … Some were hundreds of pounds, and some were as little as five pounds. The time flew by as I found myself deep down a haunted doll eBay rabbit hole.

Rob had selected and purchased the allegedly haunted doll and booked up a room at a hotel.

Did I believe any of it? Not at all. I suspect that almost all of the dolls listed on eBay as haunted [are] simply dolls that the seller has picked up from a charity shop or a car boot sale for fifty pence or a pound. [They make] up a spooky backstory and then sell them on eBay and make a healthy profit.

After Rob's experience, his mind was changed. During his experiment, he caught audio of footsteps, his recorder inexplicably stopped working, an unusual smell permeated the room, and random noises that should not have been present were caught on the device. One of the most striking events is described by Rob.

The main thing was when I awoke the morning of the second night, the doll had fallen off a chair. It was a wide chair, so it seemed odd, but the paranormal was not my immediate explanation for it. However, when I listened back to the audio I recorded through the night (which is available on my podcast), while I'm sleeping [and] snoring (a gentle snore, but you can tell I'm asleep), and in the room, there were footsteps. They get closer and louder near the recorder positioned on a table right in front of the doll sitting on the chair. Then you hear the doll's head hit the base of a lamp as it falls down.

All of this is detailed on his podcast, and Rob remains open minded.

All of this additional information leads to more questions than answers. Perhaps there's more work to be done to understand if the doll really is haunted, and if it is, by whom.

Edna and Me

Sitting beside me as I write this is Edna the Doll. Rob originally sent her to stay with me for a few weeks as an experiment, but he has, at the time of writing, allowed me to adopt her. When she arrived in the post, I was nervous. By this point, I'd been studying haunted objects and haunted dolls for a significant period of time, and I knew that there were genuine phenomena associated with Edna. I was keen to see her come out of the confines of Rob's car boot (where she'd stayed after causing creepy occurrences) and to experience home life with me, even if I was a bit wary of the potential repercussions!

Edna is a pretty, dainty little doll. Although her original listing (from where she was sold online to Rob) described her as a dark, disturbed spirit of a child, it was hard to believe it looking at her cute porcelain features and silky peach dress. Yet I know looks can be deceiving. Edna is the kind of porcelain doll that was mass produced in the 1980s. In fact, I've seen a few exact replicas of her online, so she isn't rare in terms of the doll itself. Yet a spirit can potentially link to any object, and it seems Edna is no different, as I was soon to find out.

After Edna arrived, I had some interesting experiences. Heads didn't spin, and there was no upturned furniture or demonic voices, but setting aside Hollywood expectations early on, I genuinely came to believe there was an energy attached to this doll.

When the doll first arrived, I didn't feel much of anything, though that didn't bother me. I don't consider myself psychic, and I don't have any abilities of that kind other than the fact that I've had what I consider paranormal experiences during my lifetime. I set her aside in the house after speaking aloud a warm welcome. Later that same first day, though, I was sitting in my lounge when I began to feel a very cold sensation down my right side and what I can only describe as chills and goosebumps down my right arm and leg. This continued for some time. Of course, there's no way to definitively attribute this to Edna the Doll, though to me it almost felt like a presence had sat down beside me on the sofa. To feel something so soon felt promising.

I decided to try a spirit box app on my phone whilst asking Edna questions. For the most part, when "responses" come through, it is hard to pull out words from the noise, and when you do, there's always a danger you are hearing what you want. However, there was a sequence of time when all of my questions seemed to be responded to in ways that made complete sense and seemed clear. The session went as follows:

Me: "Who is this?"
Spirit box: "Edna."
Me: "This is Edna?"
Spirit box: "Yes."
Me: "Thank you."
Spirit box: "You're welcome."
Me: "Do you miss Rob?"
Spirit box: "I do."

During one of the early days of her stay, there were a few sounds that I heard during the nighttime—sounds that I can't ordinarily say I recognise as "usual" sounds of my home. There was a series of bangs and thuds, and at one point, there was an experience of "corner of the eye" phenomena, whereby I was sure something whizzed past me whilst I was sitting down in my lounge. I looked immediately to my side and even got up to look about the room, but nothing was there. To add to this, my husband later said he saw a figure (shadowy, corner-of-the-eye movement) that he found so startling he had to look around the house to be sure no one had gotten in. The house was, of course, empty.

I continued to experiment with Edna over the coming days and weeks, as I wanted to document the experience for this project. I tried the spirit box app again, and I asked, "How are you feeling, Edna?" In response I heard what sounded like "I am happy." There was a further occasion when I said hello to the doll using the app, and a voice that sounded like it said "hello" responded. On another occasion, I tried an EVP session (whereby I used my Dictaphone and asked questions aloud). I asked Edna if she could try her hardest to say hello on my recorder.

When I played back the file on my laptop, I could hear what sounded like a "he-he-he" or small laugh or noise in response where there should have been nothing but silence. One of the most significant captures, in my opinion, was an EVP recording in which I asked Edna how old she was. On playing back the file, I heard a very faint response which sounded like "six." I had to enhance the sound, as I wanted to hear the audio as loudly as possible, and sure enough, there is what sounds like a child's voice saying "six."

I wanted to learn more about Edna. As stated previously, I am not gifted with a psychic ability, but I felt sure that this spirit had a story to tell, and I was perhaps not able to hear it. I reached out to psychic medium and author Patti Negri (whom you will hear more from in this book). Patti has worked on shows such as *Ghost Adventures* and has worked with Peggy the Doll. If anyone could sense something, I felt sure it would be Patti.

Curious and willing, Patti agreed to look at some photos of Edna alongside some of her gifted friends, and she agreed that there is indeed an attachment.

"The doll is definitely active," Patti confirmed. "We all got 'fire,'" she added, explaining that there was some kind of link to Edna perhaps being burned. "Maybe she was playing with matches or something and got lit on fire or maybe some kind of abuse [involving fire]."

Fascinated by what Patti had to say, I turned to the Spirit Talker app, and, amazingly, the words "burnt" and "desperate" appeared. It felt like the energy attached to the doll was trying to reaffirm what Patti had said.

I began scouring online to try and find other methods of communicating with spirits and haunted objects. I discovered items called *cat balls*. Originally designed for pets to play with, these little clear plastic balls light up only when touched or pushed. They are touch sensitive, meaning they make ideal tools for ghost hunters. Reading the reviews of these pet toys online highlights how they've been adopted by those interested in the paranormal: Nearly all the reviews are by ghost-hunting enthusiasts. The idea is that you set the ball in a room, or on top of an object, and call out for any energy around to touch the ball. If that happens, the ball lights up.

I decided to buy a set of these balls to experiment with Edna, and I am glad I did, for they ended up being a regular communicative tool for her and me.

I placed one of these balls on Edna's legs and regularly asked her to touch the ball using her energy. For several days, nothing happened and the ball remained inactive. Yet, one night, I placed Edna in my bedroom with the ball on her legs. I was about to go to sleep, the lights in the house were off, and suddenly the ball started flashing its lights. I said thank you to Edna, and it happened again. Incredibly, I asked her a third time if she could touch the ball, and after a few moments of darkness and silence, the ball suddenly lit up again. I felt sure Edna was present and that it was her energy making the ball active.

This was the beginning of many times when the ball would light up inexplicably whilst on or around Edna. On one particular occasion, I was lying in bed alone and was trying to sleep when I suddenly felt what I can only describe as a physical hand touching the back of my leg. It felt so definite and real, I immediately suspected it to be Edna. I was convinced more than ever that she was trying to reveal herself to me.

When I combined these phenomena with her communication and EVPs, I felt personally satisfied that Edna was in fact "haunted" and a young girl is attached to her.

After some time, I communicated with Rob about how much I'd enjoyed having the doll with me. After some further conversations, we decided Edna would remain with me. The experiment was intended to be a few weeks but ended with me permanently adopting Edna.

She still lives with me, and whilst it's still the early days, I plan on doing a lot more experimenting and communicating with her. She now feels like a little friend to me, and I look forward to what lies in store.

Bonnie

When I began the process of writing this project and putting the material together, I had an idea. The thought came to me pretty early on: I was going to trawl the listings online and purchase an allegedly haunted doll. Through the course of writing the book, I would do several experiments and investigations with it to see if I could experience anything paranor-

mal or unusual in nature. As I went along, I would note the results (if any) and share them with readers here.

As already stated, scepticism was, and still is, my starting point. I simply scoured the many dolls listed for sale, reading the description of each, and decided to take a gamble on a doll named Bonnie. The seller was someone who had a huge amount of positive feedback and is well respected in the field. Indeed, many of the customers stated that they believed their doll to be haunted and that they wouldn't buy from any other seller. Too good to be true? Possibly ...

Bonnie is a pretty little thing. Standing at approximately sixteen inches, wearing a red velvety dress, bonnet, and white shoes, she is a lovely porcelain doll. She has deep brown, realistic-looking eyes and wears her hair in long plaits. She caught my attention early on during my time searching through items for sale, and I was even more intrigued when I read her description.

Her listing labelled her as a haunted doll with positive energy, and the information section said that she contains the spirit of a twenty-seven-year-old lady from Scotland. During investigations with her, the original owners found out that she had died in a fire in the early 1900s. Bonnie is a religious soul who likes to be kept with a Bible. Although she is quite a sad spirit, she is kind and protective. Her previous owners caught paranormal activity on the spirit box when working with her.

Trusting it would make an interesting experiment, I pressed the buy button and purchased Bonnie. She arrived a few short days later. A beautiful item that, at the very least, would look good on my shelf if nothing else.

I had no rigid plans for how I was going to approach things with my experiment. My only thought was to see if I could somehow capture something interesting, whether it be through digital recordings, photos, or reputable paranormal apps. If I experienced something like a touch, smell, or sight around her, then that would, of course, be even better.

The Experiments

First of all, I downloaded an EMF app from a company that had good feedback. Electromagnetic field readers are said to indicate spikes in energy surrounding certain areas or objects. For several minutes, I placed the phone next to Bonnie with the app running and asked out loud for the spirit—if there was any—to come close and cause the EMF meter to spike. After several attempts and many minutes passed, it was clear that nothing was happening.

I then moved on to a spirit box app, which had been recommended to me by a friend. This works by sweeping through white static and radio airwaves and, apparently, picking up spirit voices audibly. With this, I had more success.

> *Me:* "Can you confirm your name for me?"
> *Spirit box:* "Bonnie."
> *Me:* "Where are you from?"
> *Spirit box:* "Glasgow."
> *Me:* "Are you happy?"
> *Spirit box:* "I am happy."
> *Me:* "Do you like being here?"
> *Spirit box:* "Yes."

To be clear, there were several questions to which I was given no answers. There were also times when it seemed that there *was* some audible noise in response, but it was hard to make out what, if anything, was being said. Noted above are the responses that seemed clear, consistent, and unusually precise.

I was surprised that I had any response at all that seemed to make sense. It certainly made me sit up and pay more attention. I am aware of the phenomenon of *pareidolia*, in which random patterns or noises can be perceived as something that makes sense when in reality they are random nonsense. I kept this in mind.

Next, I moved on to the Alice Box app, a popular paranormal application that has been used on television. The idea is to call out and then words appear on the screen, somehow manipulated through the energy of the spirit present. Again, I called out questions and had some responses.

Keeping in mind how Bonnie allegedly died in a house fire, I called out a few questions and made comments about her manner of death:

Alice Box: "Limp ahead, grass … infant … running …"
Me: "Are you talking about the time your house was on fire and your family had to escape?"
Alice Box: "Truth."
Me: "Are you religious, Bonnie? Do you like the Bible?"
Alice Box: "Scientists shove truth."

Me: "Are you angry at scientists who reject God and faith?"
Alice Box: "Often."
Me: "Thank you for talking to me, Bonnie."
Alice Box: "Okay."

It was during this time I noticed a nagging headache beginning to form, and I ended the session. I wasn't sure what to make of the responses I'd received, but I was interested enough to know I'd be trying again.

On July 28, I decided to try another session with Bonnie using some paranormal apps. Using the Spirit Talker app, I sat by the doll and began calling out questions. Like the Alice Box app, responses come up on the screen.

Me: "Are you here, Bonnie?"
Spirit Talker: "Florence."
Me: "Is that your real name?"
Spirit Talker: "Don't tell."
Me: "Are you happy?"
Spirit Talker: "I have no regrets."

I mentioned the fire and the way Bonnie is alleged to have died.

Spirit Talker: "They hear me scream."
Me: "Did you get burned in the fire, Bonnie?"
Spirit Talker: "My legs."

This was the last response I was given on the Spirit Talker app (at least that seemed to correlate to my questions), so I closed the application. I opened the Alice Box programme but received no responses. Turning instead to the spirit box, I asked about the fire again and if her legs got burnt.

The response was immediate: "Fire burnt up."

I thanked Bonnie and ended the session.

All in all, I am fascinated by the idea of Bonnie and her history. Yet the use of apps on the phone is often frowned upon and deemed untrustworthy by some in the paranormal community. I cannot say whether any responses I experienced were genuine or coincidental, but I shall continue to work with Bonnie and see if I can find out more using other techniques and resources.

CHAPTER 5
INTERVIEWS WITH OWNERS
OF HAUNTED DOLLS

So far, my journey into haunted dolls has taken me to some creepy places, yet much of what I read about the subject only led me to even more questions. I found myself with an insatiable appetite for the subject and wanted to delve into the minds and experiences of those who had hands-on experience of owning a haunted doll. What was that like? Was it anything like in the movies? I doubted it. Yet it had to be an enthralling and enchanting experience, I bargained. So, I set out on a quest to find owners from all over the world and put my questions to them. I wanted to know it all.

Kari Bergen

During my research, I found myself watching the documentary *A Haunting in Blue Hill*, an investigative show that followed a paranormal team as they studied a haunted doll. It was in this show that I first saw Kari Bergen. Kari is a paranormal investigator and collector of haunted items and is the owner of Ephemera Obscura, an online haven which sells historical and rare documents and photos. Kari shared her insight, experience, and expertise in the documentary. I reached out to her, as I wanted to discuss her insights and beliefs.

I'm an intuitive assemblage artist, paranormal investigator, and owner of Ephemera Obscura, a carefully curated collection of antique ephemera and vintage oddities. I grew up in a haunted home near Chicago, surrounded by haunted things. As a highly sensitive person, I had paranormal experiences so regularly that I didn't realize there was anything out of the ordinary going on until I started trying to talk about my experiences to others. Some of my earliest memories are ghost stories, and my first self-chosen Halloween costume at age three was a ghost.

I survived several life-threatening illnesses in my childhood, including ovarian cancer at age fifteen. I wasn't aware at the time, but looking back, it seems like my psychic sensitivities were thrown wide open and I was experiencing things I just couldn't explain. Only two years after my own brush with death, I lost my close friend Josh to cancer just before his twenty-first birthday. He let me and others know he was still around in spirit in no uncertain terms, and it was those experiences that led me down the path of paranormal investigation.

So, when did she begin collecting antiques and start to experience the haunted object phenomenon?

I've been collecting antiques since I was little. It's something we liked to do as a family. I started buying my own antiques at thirteen, and my favorite to collect were old photographs. By age sixteen, I had a decent-sized collection and decided I needed to find an old photo album to put them in. I finally found what I was looking for at a little antique store in Wisconsin. It was an empty Victorian photo album in soft blue velvet, delicate flowers painted on the front. "Empty album" was written on the inside front cover. The woman who sold it to me double-checked each page to make sure it was empty before wrapping it up in brown paper.

It sat wrapped up that way for a few months before I finally sat down to put my photo collection inside. I unwrapped the album and was remembering how lovely it was as I flipped through the empty pages until, lo and behold, there was a portrait of a trio of Edwardian teens holding diplomas tucked into one of the openings. I was certain there were no photos in this album, so I was very surprised. I assumed, though, that two pages had somehow stuck together without the cashier or me noticing. I quickly flipped through the rest of the album and assured myself there were no others. Still, how strange! I wanted to show my mom and went running over to her. When I opened the album to show her, there was a second photo tucked in the opposite page—a cabinet photo of a Victorian woman! I was absolutely stunned, but that was just the beginning.

The photos moved around the album of their own accord. I thought a family member must be playing a prank on me and devised elaborate ways of trying to catch the culprit. It didn't matter what I did; the photos and occasionally the album itself would move around even from behind a locked door.

The idea of haunted photographs fascinated me, but it didn't take long before Kari began talking about spirited dolls—the reason we got in contact in the first place.

I believe there are many ways for dolls to become different types of haunted. I'll break it down into the four main ones as I see them.

Demonic or Possessed

People often refer to dolls inhabited by or under the control of inhuman entities, or "demons," [as] *possessed*. This is the type of doll everyone is so afraid of, and thanks to their popularity in horror movies, we have plenty of terrifying imagery and scenarios to help fuel our fears. Demonic dolls are absolutely a real thing, but of all the types of haunted dolls I come across, I encounter this one the least.

Demons can attach themselves to, or "infest," dolls in a few different ways. It can be done intentionally through binding, which is a ritual to summon and attach a spirit to a doll or other object. Representing spirits in ritual is among the original purposes for dolls, so there is a long history of different ways our ancestors used dolls in connection with the spirit realm, including representing gods and deities. But more frequently, a negative inhuman attachment happens incidentally through energetic imprints, residues, or cords that resonate and connect with lower-level entities. You never know what sort of spirits have been attracted to the energies a doll has accumulated before coming into your life. Dolls that have been used in ritual and haven't been cleansed can be somewhat like a Ouija board that hasn't been closed down properly. They could contain an open portal that is letting energy or spirits into your space.

Cursed (Ritual [or] Magic)

To me, the creepiest dolls that I run into more commonly are cursed dolls. They just have a bad feeling about them. Cursed dolls carry negative energy that spills into the environment, causing people to experience bad luck, poor relationships, ill health, accidents, nightmares, and all types of unpleasant paranormal activity. Curses can happen spontaneously from the residual effects of a tragedy, such as when the soul of a murdered person releases an intense level of anguish, hatred, and rage toward a particular person, family, or group. Sometimes, this can create a *thought form*, or an entity created by thoughts combined with an emotional outpouring. Curses can also come about through bad circumstances, like having stolen something from a cemetery, trespassing in a sacred place, or having wronged a spirit.

And, of course, the most obvious [ways are] through ill will; deliberate, planned, and intended harm; anger [or] hate channelled into an innocent-looking doll and given as a gift. The eyes are truly windows to the soul, and our focused gaze, time, energy, and thoughts directed at a person, or the figure of a person, can create a thought form or curse.

Attachments

Spirit attachments are what I consider your classic haunted doll. These are dolls that have intelligent human spirits attached to them. Spirits will gravitate toward objects that were familiar to them in life, attracted by energies and emotions that resonate with their spirit. These spirit attachments can be earthbound spirits, who tend to always be present with the doll, or spirits visiting from the other side, who come and go as they please. You would think that the ghosts haunting these dolls must be the people that owned them in life, but this is often not the case. Dolls may feel familiar to a spirit because of the time period they were made in. [Or] the fashion or features resemble what the spirit looked like. [It could be that] the doll is emotionally charged with an energy that resonates with the spirit, or they may be drawn by the emotions that the doll elicits from the living. For instance, a small child that wants comfort may attach to a baby doll that is being held frequently. Or a mean spirit that gets a kick out of scaring people might pick a doll that already gives people the creeps. When we direct our attention to these dolls, and especially when we resonate with them energetically or emotionally, it is, in a sense, feeding the spirit attached.

Residual

The most common type of haunted dolls I encounter, and my favorite to collect, are residually haunted dolls. I can't go into an antique store without running into at least one. These kinds of hauntings are much more subtle, but they can radiate ill or positive effects that influence moods and behaviors. Residual hauntings are created and sustained by energetic and emotional imprints from the living. They're like an energetic recording that replays when triggered or the conditions are right. Residually haunted dolls are often dolls that were handled regularly and with a strong outpouring of emotion. But even a single event or trauma with a strong-enough outpouring of emotion leaves a "residue" that can still be felt long afterward.

For instance, a doll that was with a child when their life was taken might be imprinted with terrible fear and pain the child experienced [or] the heart-wrenching grief of their parents when they got the news. But an event doesn't need to be negative to create a residual haunting. I have a little toy dog that is imprinted with a girl's birthday party. It exudes so much joy, love, and delight that I picked it up and could not put it back down. It gives me a feeling of childish exuberance that I can only compare to meeting my first puppy. The girl who received it must have been so excited; I think she treated it like a real puppy. I also think she kept the toy for her entire life and relived that happy time every time she looked at it and held it.

I wondered whether Kari thought that haunted dolls were actually a rare occurrence, so I put the idea to her. I was surprised by her response.

Not at all! I think that the most extreme examples are relatively uncommon, but the truth is, most of us already have experience with residually haunted dolls in our homes. It's just that as adults we've forgotten all about it. Residually haunted items and dolls are everywhere, and as living people, we are creating and sustaining them on a daily basis.

Having said this, Kari goes on to explain that this doesn't mean she isn't wary of the many alleged haunted dolls that pop up in online sales.

I am both skeptical and cautious when it comes to dolls listed as haunted or possessed. I am skeptical because it's very easy to claim a doll is haunted and fake evidence of that. I have no doubt there are scammers who make false claims, but that's not why I avoid items marked as haunted online. It would be all too easy for someone selling a doll to intentionally or unintentionally create or attract a haunting by imagining or describing one for others to imagine. Even more off-putting for me is that some people may intentionally bind or trap spirits to these dolls, and I don't know what their experience level or intentions might be. For me, there are risks in accepting a haunted doll into my home without being able to read the energy first.

Kari, however, owns a number of haunted dolls, and I was especially curious to uncover how she started collecting.

I usually tell people that I don't find the dolls; instead, it seems like the dolls find me. Perhaps by word of mouth, but sometimes through amazing coincidences, I end up meeting people who need someone to help them find homes for dolls they no longer want to keep. I have rescued them from attics, basements, garages, and am often the last resort before people throw them away! I think they show up in my life because I am sensitive to the energies attached to them and I genuinely care.

Does she own a large amount of haunted dolls, then?

My doll collection started out very small. My husband hates dolls, and for his sake, I used to try to keep my collection on one shelf of my curio. Fast forward to the present day, and I've been running a doll orphanage for the last six years or so. I love helping find homes for haunted and neglected dolls. I've always been sensitive to the emotional energies of both the living and the dead. It breaks my heart to see someone's once well-loved doll be thrown in the trash. I have also seen firsthand the way a spirit responds to being cared for. Some dolls have spirits that are quite upset about how the doll they inhabit has been treated; it matters to them. Sometimes just noticing and appreciating a haunted doll seems to help spirits attached to it. Knowing that the doll will be cared for, perhaps they feel free to move on. I often find dolls that need help to be appreciated, headless dolls that still hold memories, doll heads that still tell a story, [and] dolls that need new clothes, a dab of glue, or a new wig. By running my doll orphanage, I can scoop up any doll that calls out to be seen and make sure it ends up somewhere where it will be appreciated.

With Kari's impressive depth of experience in owning and living with haunted dolls, I ask her what advice she can give to those who are looking to start their own collection. For instance, how do we know when a doll is actually haunted? How do we deal with caring for it?

The number one thing I pay attention to is my gut reaction. I pay attention to the cues my body is giving me when I look at or hold a doll. Am I having any physical reactions, like a tightening chest, a queasy feeling, sudden anxiety, sweating, [lightheadedness]? That doll is not good for me. It may look innocuous, but my body is telling me that the doll's energies are having a discordant or negative impact on me. Sometimes these things are quite subtle. A fleeting wave of nausea is easy to overlook when I'm excited about a find, but the effects may become more noticeable once I'm home. On the other hand, if I experience a warm buzzing, electric tingles, or other positive sensations, I know that my body feels comfortable or attracted to the energies in the doll. Dolls that resonate with you are telling you a story. It's important to listen to that story and decide if it's a story you want to be a part of. Just because you feel a pull doesn't mean you have to bring it home.

Regularly handling, interacting with, and shopping for haunted dolls does come with risks. If I know I will be handling haunted dolls, either while shopping or during [an] investigation, there are some practices I try to follow to help keep me safe, healthy, and connecting only with spirits that I want contact with. Most important is to be grounded, meaning well rested, fed, hydrated, and in a good frame of mind. It's never a good idea to handle haunted dolls when you are sick, tired, or in a bad mood. Negative emotions like anger, grief, and anxiety can lower your vibrations and color the intuitive info you receive. This can attract lower-level entities that resonate with (or are fed by) negative energy. The intuitive impressions you get when you're ungrounded, tired, or anxious are often confusing and inaccurate. That can be a problem if you're trying to sense how you truly feel about the energy attached to a haunted doll. You might feel drawn to a doll that is resonating with a bad mood, and later, when you are in a better mood, you may wonder why you picked it up in the first place.

Red Flags

I would avoid a doll that causes you or those in your home to have nightmares, accidents, unexplained health problems, changes in personality, uncharacteristic mood changes and behavior, or…unwanted paranormal activity.

Listening to Kari explore her experiences and memories of haunted dolls and objects has been both exciting and unnerving and makes the reality of haunted dolls feel very valid. I thank her and head off, knowing I've still got a lot of learning to do.

Emma H.

Restoring old dolls comes with a risk. I began communicating with a lady who wants to identify only as Emma H. From the UK, she has spent many years restoring antique and vintage dolls. Surprisingly, she soon found herself experiencing paranormal events around certain dolls in her care. Here, she talks to me about some of the experiences she had.

I'll just preface this by saying although I am intuitive as a person and can see and hear things and have done so my entire life, I didn't actually go out and buy these dolls for any other purpose than to learn to restore them. I had been given my nan's dolls as a little girl, but the string connecting the arms, legs, and head to the body had failed on them both, and they were a mass of parts. They were packed away, and as an adult, I got them out again and learned to string them together. Then, I discovered a whole community of people restoring their own dolls, so my love of acrylic paint, Milliput, and sandpaper was born.

My personal belief is that whatever came with these dolls are probably demonic [or] unclean spirits pretending to be children and sweet little old ladies. I don't believe for one second these entities [or] spirits were who they said they were, and I had absolutely no desire to encourage them. Although I can see and hear these things, I want and have nothing to do with them.

All of the dolls came from the same local auction house because, at the time, it was a good place to buy these dolls for cheap to learn restoration. But I did buy other dolls that didn't have any spirits attached from the same place.

Christopher

Christopher was the first doll I bought. When I got him home, I became aware of feeling like I was being watched, which at the time I didn't attribute to being from the doll. I would wake up in the night hearing a child whispering, and I ignored it. Then, one night I woke with a jump and saw a small, dark-haired boy standing by the side of the bed in front of me just staring. I swore and turned the light on, and of course, there was nothing there. I asked out loud his name and asked him what he wanted. A few days later, I woke up [at the] normal time and heard a child say, "Christopher." So that's how he got his name. I never really heard anything from Christopher again, but I do love how he seems to stand without assistance. I still have the doll, but as I've moved on from doll restoration to other things, he and Elsie (whom I'll mention next) are in plastic boxes in the shed with the others.

Elsie

Elsie the Doll was in very poor condition…After putting the doll together, resetting the eyes, and giving it a new wig, I became aware of a very strong, forceful energy around me. I got up one night to use the loo, [and] whenever I got up, I always turned the lights on and made sure everything was okay in the house. I put my head around the living room door, and at the same time, a head looked round the kitchen door; it was that of an old woman. I ran into the living room and into the kitchen, but it was empty. Not long after, I was typing on my laptop and saw something out of the corner of my eye, just to the left of the laptop. I turned my head and could see an elderly woman's face staring at me—like a mask floating in the air, the same face I saw around the kitchen door. The laptop ended up on the floor, and I ran into the garden.

Eventually, I had to come back inside because it's my house and I can't stay in the garden, but I was just aware of this energy pacing up and down the living room, and it was angry. I could feel just this anger in the room. I sat down, asked it to please stop, and if I could help it I would, but they were scaring me. I did feel the anger stop. As clear as anything, coming out of nowhere, I heard a voice say, "That's *my* doll." I asked her name, and out loud, as clear as anything, she said, "Elsie." I told Elsie that I was sorry I bought her doll, and if she wanted me to sell it, bin it, or do whatever, then I would. I then heard, "Keep it." So I did. Never heard anything again.

The Unnamed Dolls

Doll1 and Doll2 were by far the most interesting of the four just simply because of what was going on and the magnitude of activity. I bought them after Christopher but before Elsie, so after these two, I sort of knew the scores on the door with these types of dolls. They came as an auction lot together. Even walking home with them after I picked them up from the auction house, I felt like someone was walking beside me. The larger doll had a cardboard cylinder voice box that says "Mama" when the doll is moved [and] shaken, and it was going off as I was walking. At the time, I laughed and thought nothing of it. But when I got home and took the doll's head off (the doll had a cloth body), I got the voice box out of the doll, and it was broken. I shook it from side to side and nothing happened. I put it back inside the doll and sewed it back up. Things then started happening in the house. I felt [like I was] constantly being watched. I had a camera overlooking the front door; three of these cameras were nuked in a short space of time, all different brands. No other appliances in the house were affected, and I even changed the plug socket I used.

The camera randomly set off one day, and you could hear me talking to my dog and a child was answering me. I managed to save the clip, but the audio on it was messed up, and when I went back to try and save the footage off the memory card, the card had corrupted. The final time it happened, I viewed the footage [and] there was a black mist by the front door. When I tried to save the footage off it, the camera died. Even the memory card was corrupted. And my phone died as well; it was completely dead. So, I had to replace my phone as well as the camera, but I saw it.

My front door would unlock on its own, but when I watched the camera, there was nobody there, nobody outside. I came downstairs one morning to find my back door unlocked. My garden was completely enclosed and surrounded by a high fence. The lock was completely intact, nobody was in the house, nothing was taken. Nothing on the living room camera either. I would hear knocks on my bedroom door when I was in bed and a child shouting, "Mummy! Mummy!" Despite being broken, the voice box on the big doll would randomly go off as well.

Internal doors were opened and closed. I was taking a shower, and when I got out of the shower, the bathroom door was wide open. When I checked the cameras [on] the property, there was nothing showing. I put a pan on the stove to boil water, and when I got up to put the pasta in it, the gas was completely off. The dial had been turned off; I know for a fact I turned it on and lit the gas. My slow cooker was randomly turned off as well by the dial, so I came home dreaming of a stew and it was uncooked. Again, I know I put it on.

Things in the house would move around as well. I knew where I put stuff down, but when I went back, it wasn't there. I lost a ring as well; I put [it] down in a dish I usually put it in, [and] that disappeared. And I've never found it. There was regular knocking and banging. It was just bonkers. I remember just feeling really under the weather myself and just living in a fog and couldn't function. I started looking into haunted dolls, did a lot of research online, and I managed to find someone to take them both, and she happily did. I was completely honest about what had been going on, but she wasn't deterred. She said, "Oh yeah, they'll do that." I think she paid what I'd paid for them at the auction, and I posted them off. I remember packing them up, and the entire time, the voice box was going off "Mama, Mama," and I heard a child crying, like really sobbing. Walking down the road with the box to the post office, the voice box was going off. Even when the parcel was weighed at the post office, it was going off, and the staff were laughing. But I came home, and it was noticeably different in the house, a definite calm and stillness. I remember just opening all the windows and standing in the breeze as it came in just so relieved it was all over. I spoke to the woman who bought them off me; she said they got there safely, and she did some work with them. I wished her all the best.

It taught me a great lesson about what you bring into your home, and I was a lot more careful after that with the dolls I bought. If it felt a bit off, then I just didn't get them. After Elsie, I didn't have any problems.

Evelyn Hollow

I feel we are all drawing closer to understanding the reality of the fascinating yet creepy truth. I always feel drawn to learning from those who have studied such things in depth. When I first came across Evelyn Hollow, I was compelled and inspired by her stance on paranormal phenomena, much of which she shared as a regular guest on Danny Robins's hit podcast series *Uncanny*.

Evelyn is an award-winning parapsychologist and author who has been featured on TV shows and radio as well as the *Uncanny* series. Born in Scotland, she has studied all aspects of the paranormal world and has become a very respected name in the field of study. She has a particular fascination with haunted objects, and when I found this out, I had to reach out and have a conversation with her about the topic.

The first and foremost question on my mind for Evelyn was a simple one: Does she believe haunted objects, such as dolls, actually exist?

Some cultures and belief systems show a ritual practise of trapping what could be considered spirits or forms of consciousness in objects. Consider the genie in the lamp, which is based on the Islamic Jinn, or the use of dolls in Vodun or hex bottles in Western witchcraft. Psychologically speaking, if you assign vitalistic properties to an inanimate object, you'll behave as though these are true regardless of any supernatural powers.

I take this to mean haunted dolls are certainly a possible reality, but much of what many of us perceive as a haunting *could* be psychological in nature. If there are genuine occurrences of a doll being haunted, though, how does Evelyn think this occurs?

Some cultures use rituals to call or summon something and then trap it within a vessel. Some [believe] breaking an object does not end its power but simply releases it. An object's real power lies in the sociocultural impact it has on the collective minds of those that behold it.

What about the market online, which is flooded with allegedly haunted dolls? There could be many genuine sellers and dolls, but it's hard not to worry about the fraudsters who are out to make money. In this area, Evelyn is sceptical and is quite open about it.

> It's spooky capitalism. It's simply to make money, and of course, owning creepy stuff is fun, but if you're buying [or] selling it in order to create paranormal phenomena, then all you are doing is muddying the field.

Talking with Evelyn, I suggest that it's possibly quite rare to find a haunted doll by randomly trawling the internet. Does she agree? I suspect so, and she soon confirms it.

> It's very rare; it's one of the hardest aspects of my job.

She goes on to explain how she hasn't personally worked with a haunted doll.

> Not directly. I have dozens of items from haunted locations but not ones that are said to be cursed themselves.

I come away from our exchange realising how wide and varied opinions on haunted dolls are. Whilst it's been enjoyable so far—having so many people's experiences actually validate the existence of haunted objects—I know the value of stepping outside of that and hearing things from a fresh perspective. I'm sure Evelyn would agree; it's always best to have a healthy dose of scepticism.

Gemma

For some time, I have been in contact with Gemma, who runs a company called Junior Paranormal Events. She has written regular content for my website, The Haunted Attic, and various other publications. She spends a lot of her time organising paranormal events and investigations for the younger generation of ghost hunters, and on top of this, she owns a haunted doll. In early 2024, she opened

Gemma's Doll, Hannah

herself up to "adopting" an allegedly haunted doll named Hannah. With some of the incredible experiences Gemma and her family [have] had with the doll, I couldn't resist having a chat about it.

I wondered how it came about that Gemma ended up buying a haunted object.

My honest answer is that I still do not know, and I still can't fathom what happened that day back in

November 2023. We went to Haworth, Yorkshire, for my daughter's birthday. It is full of really quirky shops, and we have been a few times. This time, there was a new shop we hadn't been in before. It had lots of random objects, supposedly with stories connected to them, including lots of dolls. They were arranged on shelves dotted around. My daughter has always been fascinated with "haunted dolls," and she was happily pottering around looking at them all.

At this point, I couldn't help but ask if Gemma liked collecting dolls.

I do not like dolls whatsoever; I never have, but I was drawn to a doll sat on the fireplace in the corner of the shop. I was told that she was called Hannah and that she was looking for a new home.

Fast forward a couple of hours and Hannah is wrapped up in purple tissue paper, sat on my lap in the car on the way home. I am told by believers in haunted dolls that they often choose their owners, and I do genuinely believe that was the case with Hannah, but I really can't explain it. What I do know is that I never intentionally set out that day to acquire a doll, haunted or otherwise, but Hannah had other ideas.

Did she believe that dolls could be haunted at that point? Gemma wasn't convinced in the past before Hannah.

I know people roll their eyes when the topic of haunted dolls is brought up—I was one of those people. Even when being at My Haunted Hotel, seeing dolls come flying off the shelves, I was still not convinced by the concept of a haunted doll. But then Hannah came into my life. Initially, so convinced was I that she was positively not haunted, I put her in my living room. To put this into context, I am a paranormal investigator, and I do not bring any equipment or conduct investigations in my home because that is our safe space. However, within just a few hours of her being there, things started to happen which even my sceptical husband could not explain. There were footsteps heard running around on the upstairs landing, the sound of a girl laughing outside our bedroom door in the middle of the night, and my husband and I having the same weird dream of a young girl trying to speak. It got so weird that I ended up wrapping Hannah back up and putting her in the boot of the car in the early hours of the morning. She was then taken up to our office at Champness Hall, where she now lives.

With Gemma stating such incredible phenomena occurred once she adopted Hannah, I was curious about other paranormal events surrounding the doll.

> She has moved on several occasions—one of which we … caught on video when out filming with our team. She sometimes gets strange marks on her face; they appear from nowhere and then disappear. We have had black marks, and then there was an occasion where she was out on location with us and was alone in the basement where she got a blue paint-like mark on her face. Her hair seems to have a life of its own. I can leave her in the evening and her hair is smoothed down into a side sweep; when I come back the next morning, it looks as though she has been on an adventure—all stuck up and unkempt looking. She has a personality all … her own and can be very chatty; we communicate using equipment. My goodness, she lets you know if she doesn't like something, and we always have to say good morning and good night to her.

With that level of activity from the doll, it made me wonder if Gemma was nervous around Hannah.

> When I initially got her, absolutely! I wondered what on earth was happening and what I had done

by bringing Hannah home with me. However, we have all bonded with her now, and she has become part of the family—that sounds weird I know. My son loves her, and I constantly find sweets on my desk that he has left for her. My daughter draws pictures for her, our dog likes to give her the occasional lick on the face, and the whole team has really got a soft spot for Hannah. One of our Boo Crew members likes to carry Hannah around wrapped up inside her coat so that she doesn't get cold, [and] our Junior Ambassadors insisted that Hannah was given a piece of birthday cake at our anniversary get-together. Hannah comes out on events with us, and she gets a lot of attention from the public—we were actually stopped by a member of staff at one location. She recognised Hannah from social media and wanted to say hello. It's very sweet!

Does Gemma own any other haunted objects, or would she consider homing any others?

Funnily enough, since getting Hannah, we seem to have become a magnet for people with dolls they no longer want! We have since acquired five more dolls that have come to us via a member of the team. They are Lucy, Mandy, Annabel, Victoria, and Mavis. But there is a strict hierarchy in our office; they all live in a glass cabinet, and only Hannah is allowed on the desk and out on an event with us. I think it is important to be open minded. The paranormal is a field where we can never know all the answers, and so I am intrigued with the idea of haunted objects. I have Hannah to thank for that. But I would draw the line at anything that is reported to be "cursed" or "evil." Whilst I don't necessarily believe in that, I have learnt my lesson from Hannah in that you just never know.

I end my conversation with Gemma feeling glad we spoke about Hannah the haunted doll for this project. To hear of an active, ongoing haunted object in such vivid detail is invaluable to those of us who want to learn about spirited dolls. I say bye to Gemma for now, hoping that Hannah behaves herself.

Whilst Gemma is on the receiving end of buying a haunted doll, I wanted to discuss the idea of selling haunted items to the public and all that it entails. I reached out to two sisters who have made quite a splash in the world of haunted dolls—and for good reason.

Supernatural Sisters

The Supernatural Sisters, Cat and Ali, have owned and studied haunted dolls for many years. From a young age, they had paranormal experiences and family members who collected haunted items. Eventually, they branched out into studying, selling haunted items, and promoting their knowledge on the subject. I read about their work when they were featured in *Cosmopolitan Magazine* and knew I had to discuss their experiences with them.

I began by asking them how the business began for them both. I'm always curious about this, because haunted objects don't seem like the most obvious thing to get into as kids.

> We have been involved in the paranormal since a very young age. All our family collected haunted items and also attached spirits to items to bring back to their own museums. Our parents died at a very young age, and we were raised by our aunt. She was the one who got us involved and interested in all things paranormal.

Having spent so much of their life engrossed in the subject, they must have had contact with hundreds of haunted items. I wondered what the most haunted object was they'd experienced so far.

> This is a hard question, as we have experienced a lot of activity over the years with all our spirits. I would say the one that sticks out the most for us would be Jolly. He is a clown that is part of Ali's personal collection, and he is active daily.

Clowns are something that unnerve a lot of people, I know, even if they are not haunted. Yet what about dolls—do they come into contact with many haunted ones?

> We have had many experiences with haunted dolls. The most interesting ones I would say are the sexual ones and also the poltergeists. They are both very active, especially at night when you are most vulnerable. We have seen dolls move. Their expressions change on film. Shadows … cling to them. A doll is the closest thing a spirit can get to a body that is not human. This, we feel, is why a spirit would be drawn more to a doll.

That's an interesting idea to me, that perhaps spirits may be drawn to dolls because they are like mini versions of the people they used to be, with physical bodies that remind them of their own.

I then ask the sisters the one question I never tire of asking because I feel it is at the heart of the matter: How do they believe dolls become haunted?

> Some spirits want to carry on in this world and don't want to move on to their next journey. Attaching themselves or getting help to attach to a doll or another object helps them remain here with us until they are ready to go to their next place. Not

all spirits want to be attached to something and will refuse. We always support this.

How can people shop for haunted objects safely? Knowing that the sisters sell spirited dolls regularly, they must have insight on what to look out for.

We would advise to ask the seller if you can see a video of their museum and own personal collections. We have several haunted museums, and we upload videos of them on a weekly basis. To make sure you are getting something genuine, always ask questions to the seller. Is there any evidence of the doll being haunted? What experiences has the seller experienced?

If someone has already purchased a doll they believe to be haunted, what would be the best way to verify that the item is genuinely spirited and that energy is attached?

We advise to look out for the little things such as different smells around you, taps and knocks, whispers. It's rarely like the movies, and people should not expect that. We would suggest that you use good, reliable ghost hunting equipment to do your own investigations with a haunted doll. It can take a long time for a spirit to let you know they are there, so patience is absolutely the best tool to have.

Not everyone who buys an allegedly haunted item is a sensitive or medium, so I ask the sisters what they recommend people use to make contact with the spirit.

> Each spirit may communicate in different ways. We use a different range, but we like to use a REM pod and trigger objects the most.

It was during the last stages of editing this book when I saw that the Supernatural Sisters had made available a doll called Knock Knock Harry. I was intrigued.

According to the sisters, Knock Knock Harry is the spirit of a boy aged thirteen, who died in the 1920s. Two twins, known personally to Ali when she was younger, had been playing in a graveyard and the spirit of Harry followed them home. Soon after this, all manner of disturbances happened in the family home. The spirit of Harry was safely attached to the vessel of a clown doll and then housed in their haunted museum.

I read about the case and couldn't help myself. I reached out to the Supernatural Sisters and agreed to adopt Knock Knock Harry. Am I mad for doing so? At the time of writing this, I await his arrival. Time will tell what will happen when he reaches me.

Ending my conversation with Cat and Ali of the Supernatural Sisters, I start to think about the psychics and mediums of the world who deal with objects like this every day.

How do they deal with haunted items, and what do they have to say about how such cases evolve and occur?

My mind goes immediately to Patti Negri—psychic, author, podcast host, and paranormal expert. If there's somebody who will have personal insight on this subject, I am sure it is her. I reach out to her, and we put a date and time in the diary. We want to talk about it in depth.

Patti Negri

Patti Negri is a well-respected psychic medium who has worked with some of the biggest names in the paranormal world and has starred regularly on the *Ghost Adventures* TV show. She is a bestselling author and has been teaching people across the world through her online courses. Patti is the owner of a haunted doll herself and has also worked with Peggy—the infamous doll that is now housed in Zak Bagans's Haunted Museum.

Patti Negri's Doll, Belle

I begin by asking Patti how her involvement in the paranormal began.

The paranormal has always been a part of my life, but it was a very private part of my life. I was involved in the entertainment industry, and I owned and ran a very corporate-oriented production company that created shows for very mainstream companies like Mattel, Microsoft, and major banks. I just figured that if these people knew that I talked to dead people on one hand and danced around bonfires in a cape on the other hand, they would not necessarily want me to be teaching ethics or sales techniques to their HR department via a song and dance extravaganza.

So how did the situation evolve since she had kept things private for so long?

I got a call from somebody who knew my private and spiritual life requesting one of my séances for their reality show. [They knew about] the way that I lift the veil, [so] people would be able to experience it and even see it on camera. I immediately said no, that is my private life, thank you, but no thank you. They literally almost begged me, and we went back and forth. All the while, I am looking at my very empty work calendar as I started to cave a bit. So, I asked them the name of the show. They said it's called *Mobile Home Disaster* and it's on Country Music Television. After a rather long pause and restraining a giggle, I thought to myself, Who in the world would watch something called *Mobile Home Disaster* on Country Music Television? (Little did I know, it would be everybody.) So, I decided to do it. It was the most fulfilling, fun, magical experience I had had in a long time. I was able to help a human little girl that everybody thought was crazy because she was drawing portals on the ceiling of her motor home, and I assured them that she was not crazy; there were just portals on the ceiling of her mobile home. I was able to help a spirit cross over that was stuck and, equally exciting, open the minds a bit of the Southern, conservative cast and crew on the shoot.

After that, her life took a very distinct turn, I'm guessing?

Yes. Since then, because I am in the middle of Hollywood, I am legitimate, I am good at what I do, and I know production from both sides, I sort of became the go-to person to call for television, speaking events, consultations, paranormal conventions, and all things paranormal. It was the best thing I ever did.

I ask Patti to explain when she realised she had a gift for contacting and communicating with spirits, and she opens up about it with ease.

I have been connecting and communicating with spirits since I could talk. I remember being a toddler and having full conversations with spirits and getting real information that I related back to my mom. I thought that was just normal procedure that everybody could do. I honestly think that most kids do have the gift of seeing spirits; it just unfortunately gets taught out of us in our modern, Western, nonmystical, completely left-brain-focused society. Luckily, it didn't get taught out of me. My mom always just said, "Yeah, Grandma could do that too!" I literally did my first séance when I was seven or eight years old. I was in my suburban Los Angeles–area home and was obsessed with talking to dead people. It was never morbid, dark, or negative. I just knew they had a lot to say.

One of the most exciting things Patti has been involved with has been the *Ghost Adventures* show, and I am eager to hear about her experience on the series.

I absolutely love working with Zak and the guys. I have been doing a couple episodes a year for the last nine years. I think I am at fifteen or sixteen episodes with the one I just filmed while writing this. Zak, Aaron, Jay, and Billy feel like brothers to me. It is always an adventure and a challenge and some of the most fun I could even imagine. They are funny, respectful, and always keep a close protective watch over me. The entire crew is great. Since they want the best and purest of my mediumship and psychic skills, I never know where we are going or what we will be investigating. Whether I am "feeling out" a space for them, doing a séance, or doing a ritual to raise the veil, I am able to go to some of the spookiest and most haunted places in the world and yet have a great team beside and behind me.

I then steer the conversation into the realm of haunted dolls, the reason we are both here. Does Patti believe dolls can be haunted?

Yes, I 100 percent believe dolls and other objects can be haunted. A disembodied spirit can take up residency almost anywhere. But, if I was a spirit looking for a vessel to live in, I would certainly much prefer a doll that had eyes and a nose and ears and mouth than a teapot or iron. Eyes represent vision; ears, hearing. A mouth gives them a voice. I am actually not sure [of] the process of how it occurs except that everything is energy. We are energy, spirit is energy, and energy seems to do well when it has a landing spot. There are certainly lots of ghosts and disembodied spirits out there without a vessel to live or hang out in, but those that find a nice doll to live in certainly get a lot more focus and attention if that's what they are looking for.

I then recall reading that Patti owns her very own haunted doll, called Belle, and I eagerly ask her to tell me more about it.

My beautiful Belle is a one-hundred-and-ten-year-old German doll who was sent to me by a girl in Belgium. She had watched me on the television show *Deadly Possessions*, which is a spin-off of *Ghost Adventures*, where Zak Bagans featured haunted objects. He had brought me in to do a séance with the infamous Peggy the Doll. The woman in Belgium figured if I could handle Peggy, I could certainly handle Belle. Belle had made her and her young daughter sick for the last couple years that she had owned her, and she did not know what to do with her. She contacted me and asked my permission if she could send her to me, and I, of course, said yes. I knew I would have the skill and training to banish any negative spirit and intuitively sensed that there was a beautiful and positive spirit in Belle as well. The magic started happening the moment she arrived. I had never done a Facebook live video before; I had never even thought about it. But for some reason, I thought I should do one of opening the box that Belle was sent in. Literally fifty thousand people watched that video. I do not have anywhere near that many followers. It was all Belle calling them in.

Once open, I immediately sensed the dark spirit and knew I had to banish it before the sun set. As much as I love haunted things, my house is my sanctuary, and I won't allow anything dark or negative in it. I did a cleansing and clearing ceremony and put Belle in a safe place to see what developed. Within days, the sweet little girl spirit within started to show herself. I still had to keep extra protection around her for months. I would keep a little bag of rue in her hand and by her side for protection because she really drained energy [from] anyone who came near her. But that drain soon wore off, and she became an important and well-loved part of our family. I watched as my dog and cat went from avoiding her at all costs to hanging out with her as much as possible. It was a beautiful transition.

Belle sounds incredible, undeniably so, but how did Patti personally verify she had a haunted doll on her hands?

It was definitely intuitive on my part, but honestly, everyone could tell. She has a personality. You actually see her face change with her moods. Three people could walk in at different times and all make the same statement about how she was feeling that day. People have seen her move on camera when she sits behind me when I am teaching my Zoom classes online. She makes her desires and needs known to anyone who comes in contact and pays attention to her, whether they consider themselves a psychic or intuitive or not. She's just that strong.

I still wonder, though, how rare it is for a haunted doll like Belle to actually exist, and Patti wastes no time in expressing her thoughts on the topic.

I honestly don't think it is that unusual for a doll to become spirited. It has been written and talked about throughout history and in every culture and belief system. Spirits inhabiting inanimate objects is just a part of life.

I ask Patti if she's had other brushes with haunted objects over the years. I was not disappointed with her response.

I have had many experiences with haunted items over the years between my strong intuition and involvement in the paranormal. It's just a part of my life. One that stands out, though, is another doll that I had. It had been given to me by a rock star friend. I had it for two years, and it sat happily in my office and was fine. All of a sudden, I noticed I was avoiding spending time in my office.

I knew something had changed. I looked around and went right to the doll. It had definitely picked up a negative spirit. I immediately contacted Zak Bagans and asked him if he wanted it for his Haunted Museum in Las Vegas. I told him it was way too haunted for me and thought that his museum would be the perfect place for a darkly haunted, very active doll. I sent him a photo, and he immediately knew it was a nail fetish doll and said he wanted it. I gifted it to him the very next day at his museum. The tour guides told me it started acting up the very first night it was there. It sits in the hallway in a cabinet, and I think it found the perfect home.

I am aware that Patti knows Jayne Harris of *Help! My House Is Haunted* and has spent time with Peggy the Doll. I couldn't resist getting Patti to open up about this.

Peggy definitely has a negative spirit attached, leaning towards demonic. I also think she is very misunderstood. When I go visit her at the museum now, I always go in with respect and greet her and tell her how beautiful she looks, and she immediately starts cursing at me through the spirit box that Zak has set up for her in her room. It's kind of funny and spooky at the same time.

Before we end our conversation, Patti parts with these words, which I feel are vital to those who are interested in owning spirited objects.

Haunted dolls are great. They can add a whole new dimension to your home and family. But I definitely recommend getting a positively haunted doll. Negative dolls … are not as much fun as they seem. They truly can cause chaos and illness and unhappiness in a home. Happy and positive haunted dolls will bring joy and will still have the spooky factor if that's what you're looking for. Check out the seller; there are a lot of fake haunted dolls out there. Use your intuition and always check reviews. I honestly think that you can have as good of luck finding a haunted doll at a thrift store or antique store if you allow yourself to trust your intuition. Then for the care and feeding of the doll, check out my book *Dollcraft: A Witch's Guide to Poppet Magick & Haunted Dolls* [from] Llewellyn books.

Leaving Patti behind, I am left pondering those amongst us who have already taken the plunge in buying a haunted object and are left regretting it, for whatever reason. With this in mind, I head over to Unsettling Toys, where there are two special individuals who spend their time rehoming unwanted haunted items.

Sara and Brian

Imagine this: You have a doll or toy in your house and you decide that it's just too creepy to keep, or perhaps you get the feeling it is haunted or cursed. At the same time, it doesn't feel quite right to simply throw the item in the bin. After all, what if the suspected energy attached decides to linger anyway? How can we deal with such items?

Lucky for us, there's a couple, Sara and Brian, who run the Unsettling Toys company. They take in dolls, toys, and unusual items from all across the world from people who want to rid themselves of haunted or unsettling items. They take them in and then match them with an owner who wants to buy or collect such objects. Sound interesting? It did to me. So, I invited Sara and Brian for an interview to find out more.

I wanted to know how Unsettling Toys started, because the idea of a company that rehomes troublesome items really fascinated me. It's not something I'd ever heard of before.

Unsettling Toys was Brian's idea. We were talking one day, and he noticed an unsettling doll that someone had given us sitting on the bookshelf.

112

Brian said, "Someone should make a company that removes creepy dolls and finds them new homes." It was just a funny passing thought until Brian's fiftieth birthday. That was when I created the business as his gift. I made the website, the Instagram, business cards, and stickers. We definitely started this endeavour with a sense of humor, but we learned very quickly that this was a much-needed service with more complexity than we ever could have imagined. Mountains of packages started arriving in the mail, and they came with stories that were terrifying, heartwarming, hilarious, or horribly sad. We feel very honored that our clients share the private details of their lives and their losses with us.

There seem to be three main reasons people send us toys: love, guilt, and fear. Sometimes, clients love a toy but need to rehome it, and they want to make sure it goes on to be loved by someone else. Sometimes, they inherit a doll, or the doll was gifted by a loved one, so they feel that they can't throw it away, but it is unsettling to them. In this case, guilt drives them to contact us. Finally, some clients send us toys instead of throwing them away or giving them to a thrift shop because they feel that the doll is haunted, and they fear retaliation or a curse. We love that we can help give all three types of clients peace of mind.

Would most of the toys that the couple deal with be considered haunted?

> We never guarantee whether a toy is haunted or not. There have been toys that we believed were just objects, and their new owners reported an active attachment, and there have been dolls with horrendous backstories and strange occurrences whose new owners felt nothing. We have found that just like with people, every doll and human interaction is unique. People and toys can "click" or "flop" just like people can click or flop with other people. That is one of the reasons that we love doing in-person events. When someone can hold the toy they are considering, they can often make their decision immediately. Lots of people choose to do remote psychic readings over Zoom if they are unable to visit in person.
>
> We also believe that toys, even if there is no entity attached, can hold memories of the past. Whether it is a feeling, or something you perceive with another sense like smell, sight, or touch, most people react in some way to our older toys that have a lot of history.

I wanted to know if the couple had their own methods for verifying if an object is haunted, so I approached the subject with them.

Above everything else, we respect the stories that people share with us when sending us a toy. We are always very careful to share the stories accurately and not allow our own experiences or beliefs to color the interpretation.

Once a toy is with us, we often work with psychics to help us identify attachments. Neither of us identifies as psychic, so we like to bring in experts. Sometimes, they report very specific attachments, and sometimes they just get a general idea of whether a haunted toy has positive, playful, negative, sad, mischievous, or angry types of energy. Many of our followers on social media have playfully teased us about how being in love, and not being particularly psychic, may be protecting us from some scary energies that can't quite get a grip on us. One person said we are like spiritual Teflon!

We definitely take note of anything unusual that happens in our home while the toy is there. We have experienced seeing movement out of the [corners] of our eyes, smoke alarms or alarm clocks going off without reason, electronics frying, strings of very good or very bad luck, a car window rolling down on its own, vivid and specific nightmares, and toys falling over or moving at very unexpected times.

Lastly, we take into account how the public inter-
acts with a toy. Sometimes, it becomes clear that
many people have similar feelings about a particular
toy. Sometimes, a very average-looking toy can draw
the attention of tons of passersby.

On my journey into studying haunted dolls, I have been
inclined to think that a haunted object is quite a rare thing.
Would the couple agree?

I think that depends on how you define *haunted*.
I think it also depends on the person perceiving the
haunting. Some people are definitely more aware of
energies and attachments than others. Many of our
toys may have memories and energies attached to
them. As far as our psychics reporting attachments
of actual spirits of people who have passed, that is
less common. Reports of more malicious nonhuman
attachments have happened too, but that is even less
common.

With my attention primarily on haunted dolls rather than
haunted objects in general, I wanted to explore if spirited
dolls were something they came across often.

I guess the short answer is yes. People frequently
send us dolls with histories of hauntings. People

have experienced hearing voices or someone calling their name, children or animals being obsessed with or terrified of the doll, seeing shadow people or movement near the doll, extended bad luck, feelings of nausea or fear around the doll, illness or death of pets or loved ones, feelings of dread or nightmares about the doll, technology failures, and more. For some, it can be very traumatic, but for others it is exciting. Many people who send us dolls are very glad for confidentiality. Their experience of a haunting may not fit well with their former beliefs, and they are afraid that their friends and families may worry or even judge them. There have been professionals, celebrities, and many skeptics who have sent us toys.

What, would they say, is the most unusual or most haunted doll they have ever sold?

Gosh, we've had some weird ones! Once, we had a haunted yo-yo! Generally, I think the most unusual ones are the handmade and personalized ones. We have an apple-head peddler woman who is very intense to look at. Once, we received caricatures of a woman's ex-boyfriends. We have faceless dolls, dolls who arrive with their hands bound and surrounded by herbs, very old dolls that look like the haunted dolls in movies but have wonderful positive energy, and dolls that look completely unremarkable but have horrifying histories.

One woman worked in hospice for many years, and she would come home and use her collection of pull-string Shrinkin' Violette dolls for support after difficult days. She drove ten hours to hand deliver some of the Violette dolls to us. They look quite unsettling, especially when they are talking, but they are full of positive energy and love.

One idea that we promote is that physical differences alone are not scary. Conjoined twins are not scary, eye differences are not scary, limb or skin differences are not scary. That then begs the question, What is scary? We think about this a lot, and the answers can range from silly and fun to downright depressing. The unknown, the aging process, injuries, being forgotten, malice, and death are a few things that can be scary. Examining the hidden parts of one's own mind can be positively terrifying. I'm sure you can tell, I love to talk about this topic.

After hearing all of this, I was curious to know what unusual or weird experiences the couple have had with haunted dolls.

It is hard to choose! There have been five dolls that were too much for us. In many of these cases, we have contacted experienced practitioners who we believe are equipped to handle a possible negative attachment.

One doll came to us with a history of causing nightmares, feelings of dread, and sleep paralysis in multiple people. Once we received him, four different smoke detectors went off on three different days, at two different homes, always at 3 a.m. or 3 p.m. The doll had a goat face, and I had very vivid nightmares about a chupacabra crawling in my second-story window.

Another doll came to us with stories of a child hearing their name called at night. When the child was three, the doll had fallen and broken a leg. The child had an accident on a trampoline the next week and broke their same leg in the same place! For a while, we had the doll's broken leg in Brian's truck and the rest of the doll inside our house. The truck window started rolling itself down! We both witnessed it happen several times. I was so mad at Brian because cars and driving are not the time or place to experiment with hauntings! Once the leg rejoined the doll, the truck window never rolled itself down again. When my kids reported having nightmares about the doll, we quickly found her a new home.

Those stories are scary, but there are positive hauntings too. Several times we have received dolls that were beloved and their owners had passed away. We have experienced heightened senses, peaceful or happy feelings, and good luck.

Do they have any words of advice for people who are looking into buying a haunted object?

My best advice is to plan carefully and make sure to communicate with others in your home. When people adopt toys without considering other people and pets in the household, the toys often return to us. Remember, one person's new bestie can be another person's literal nightmare!

What do their family and friends make of such a unique interest?

Our friends and family have been very supportive. They definitely do not all understand why we love unsettling toys so much, but knowing that we love it is enough for them. Although, when Brian hides doll heads in the microwave at work, they may have second thoughts.

Finally, I wanted to know if either of them has had an experience that made them wary or consider stepping back from dealing with unsettling toys?

Just walking into our garage and seeing thousands of tiny eyes staring at us can be a bit intense. Fortunately, nothing yet has been scary enough to make us consider quitting. We are lucky to know many experienced practitioners who can take toys from us if we ever feel out of our depth. We appreciate and honor each toy and its history. We love them for their quirks and differences, not despite them.

Miki York

Miki York is a popular ghost hunter who has a fascination with haunted dolls. After coming across his social media pages online, I discovered he had his own personal brush with creepy dolls. I wanted to know more, and thankfully Miki was excited to share his experiences.

I've always been interested in haunted dolls. The thought that an object could hold a spirit or an attachment was fascinating to me. Obviously, you hear the stories of Annabelle or Robert, but could others be the same? I got my first "haunted doll" back in 2013, and she was called Satan Sadie. She was known to be surrounded by black shadows and footsteps. I got her from a lady who had just passed away. She was a collector, and her son took over her estate. There [were] about six haunted dolls in this collection, and the son wanted to get rid of them. She had kept a diary of each of the dolls and the activity associated with each of them. Unfortunately, the son kept [that, as it was] handwritten by his mother.

I then got into collecting others to see if they also could be haunted. I next got a male doll called Posh Edward; he was an interesting doll. He would stop my spirit box from working properly and once even shut it off and no sound would come out. I had many issues when filming with Edward. I had a few other haunted dolls along the way, but I didn't really have the time to work with them. Then [along came] the infamous Janet the Doll. I had a friend in Texas who had contacted me back in 2016 and said she had a doll that all of her family hated and wanted to get rid of. She offered to send the doll to the UK free of charge; she just wanted it gone. When I received the doll, I noticed straight away she had no eyes but she did have teeth. I thought this was quite strange. She was made of leather and porcelain and had a date stamp on her back that read 1903. She had come to me with no name, and so I went straight for my spirit box to see what information I could get and to find out if she was haunted.

After a few minutes of asking her name, I finally got an answer: Janet. It was so clear, and from that day, Janet the Doll was born. I have taken her to events over the years. She has caused people to feel sick; [they get] headaches and even chest pains when in her company. She definitely has a negative feeling that comes from within her.

Miki York's Doll, Janet

I have been told by two different mediums [that] there are two spirits attached to the doll: a young girl and a man who is like her watcher. It's been said that the girl spirit was forced into the vessel using dark rituals. This could be why people feel unwell around her; she is angry and scared.

She currently sits in my bedroom, now in a case with pictures of her previous homes in America and pictures of all of her newspaper and online articles. Her story has been on … *Darkness Radio* in the States, and people to this day do not like being around her. Does it bother me? No, I kind of leave her alone unless I'm working with her, which I do from time to time. She does give me headaches when making contact with her. Are you brave enough to hold Janet the Doll?

CHAPTER 6
DOLLS IN FILM

Whilst the first part of this book focuses on the alleged true-life cases of haunted dolls and their history, the second part focuses on films and books that use the haunted doll trope for inspiration. If you enjoy a horror film or creepy read, this next section will hopefully serve as a guide for what to check out next.

When people talk about evil dolls in the horror genre, often the first thing that springs to mind are the obvious, incessant killers, such as Chucky, who have a thirst for blood and are on constant rampage to impose violent carnage. Yet my journey in compiling this book has opened my eyes to the many layers that these dolls can bring to the movie world, where graphic death scenes and violence are merely back-drops for something far more deeply human than we may at first appreciate. The dolls of these disturbing films are often representative of human torment and distress—they are often innocent-looking symbols of something dark about the human psyche.

When *Magic* was released in 1978, it was obvious the thing that was going to creep audiences out far more than anything else was the wide-eyed and unsettling ventriloquist doll known as Fats. Yes, there is something genuinely scary about ventriloquist dummies; it's undeniable. There is even a name for the phobia (a fear that isn't even that uncommon): *automatonophobia.*

In one article, written by Eleesha Lockett for website Healthline, the writer explains it like this:

> Automatonophobia is a fear of human-like figures, such as mannequins, wax figures, statues, dummies, animatronics, or robots. The fear of these figures can develop from a traumatic personal experience, or due to a variety of genetic or environmental factors.[34]

So, for those frightened of dolls (in any style, shape, or form), they have a name for their deep-rooted fear.

Magic, starring Anthony Hopkins, used the ventriloquist dummy to great effect, for Fats was certainly uncomfortable to watch, yet beyond that, the true horror lies in the central character's mental illness, which is explored through his use of the dummy. As was seemingly intended by the director and writer of the production, Fats becomes the outlet for the

---

34. Eleesha Lockett, "Understanding Automatonophobia: Fear of Human-Like Figures," reviewed by Timothy J. Legg, Healthline, November 12, 2019, https://www.healthline.com/health/anxiety/automatonophobia.

darkness of Hopkins's character, so rather than the disquieting themes of the film being because of the doll itself, it is merely a vehicle for the unfolding drama and horror.

We see the same result in psychological horror film *May* from 2002. Written and directed by Lucky McKee, *May* uses the creation of a doll as the mere outlet for a chain of dark events. Yet again, the doll itself in the movie may look creepy and sit at the centre of the unfolding plot, but it is truly May's (played by Angela Bettis) descent into darkness and madness that produces the true horror in the story. Driven by loneliness and desperation, May is a broken person who uses the doll as an outlet.

In A. D. Calvo's *The Melancholy Fantastic* from 2011, we see character Melanie Crow suffering from loss, grief, and depression. The way in which she clings to the life-size doll that she spends her lonely days with is a mirror of her disturbed mind.

Quite often, dolls used for the scare factor in horror films are the insane, demented beings that we enjoy watching for entertainment, much like Chucky. Yet as this journey into dolls in film shows, there is often something far more telling in the storylines: the true living nightmare of an individual's broken mind, of living alone and searching for salvation where there is often none to be found.

Follow me as I take a deep dive into haunted and cursed doll movies.

The Child's Play Franchise (1988–)

What better place to start than Chucky? Everybody knows Chucky, the murderous Good Guy doll who sprang to infamy in 1988 when the first film of the Child's Play franchise was released. Based on a story created by horror mastermind Don Mancini, Child's Play would go on to become one of the most significant series in horror history.

Child's Play tells the story of notorious serial killer Charles Lee Ray, who, after being hunted down by police, finds himself hiding out in a closed toy store late one night. As police on his trail get closer to finding him, Ray, who seems to have knowledge of the occult, grabs a cute Good Guy doll from a shelf and chants a spell. This results in his soul entering the doll—and so begins a journey of bloody rampage as Chucky the doll springs to life, ruining whoever gets in his way.

In the original movie, Chucky the doll is given as a gift to Andy Barclay, a young boy who is celebrating his birthday. According to the film mythology, Charles Lee Ray needs to inhabit the person he first reveals himself to. Thus begins the overarching plot of the film series: Chucky needs to possess Andy. Child's Play was a hit from the beginning, and there have been seven films in the franchise (at the time of writing) and a TV series offshoot.

Chucky evolved as the villainous doll from his humbler beginnings in the late '80s. In the first movie, Chucky didn't speak or move for most of the film, and it is only toward the end that we hear his voice and see him spring to life. As later films develop his character, we hear more speech from him, and the doll becomes far more "animated." *Child's Play 1–3* (1988–1991) were produced in a similar style; however, things soon changed for the killer doll.

In 1998, Chucky experienced somewhat of a revival in the release of the horror-comedy *Bride of Chucky*. This new addition to the franchise saw Chucky reunited with his lost love, Tiffany, who finds herself also trapped in the body of a doll. It appeared that with *Bride of Chucky* there was a new style and approach to the story. The killing scenes seemed to be far gorier, a deeper history of killer Charles Lee Ray was revealed, and there were moments of dark humour amidst the killing sprees. *Bride of Chucky* led the way for two more films starring Tiffany the doll: *Curse of Chucky* and *Cult of Chucky*.

Chucky went on to become such a huge horror icon through the years that hordes of merchandise became available, with many collectible Chucky dolls and even Tiffany dolls released. Fans were able to have a slice of horror in their own homes—if they dared…

The Child's Play story was developed and written by Don Mancini, an American director and screenwriter. As a lifelong horror fan, he studied film at UCLA.

Andy Barclay—who has starred in all but one of the Child's Play movies from the franchise—is played by actor Alex Vincent. Chucky is voiced by Brad Dourif (in later films, his daughter Fiona would join the cast). In *Bride of Chucky*, we saw the addition of American actress Jennifer Tilly, who played Chucky's sidekick, Tiffany (who is now a much-loved, staple character in the Child's Play world).

Interview with Director Don Mancini:
The Man Behind Child's Play

Don Mancini was born in America in 1963. He grew up an avid horror fan, soaking up childhood favourites such as *The Twilight Zone* and *Trilogy of Terror* (which reportedly became seeds of inspiration for his Child's Play series). Mancini studied film at UCLA in the early '80s, and in the latter half of the same decade, he began writing the first *Child's Play* film, which was released in 1988.

Mancini's filmography includes the Child's Play franchise (although not the 2019 reboot), and he was involved in writing episodes for *Tales from the Crypt* and *Hannibal*.

For this project, Don Mancini spoke with me about the development of the Child's Play world and what inspired him to keep going over the years.

The Child's Play franchise goes all the way back to the '80s, which is, of course, amazing. I wondered how that felt to Don to have created something so legendary and loved in the horror genre.

> I feel increasingly grateful, I would say. It's thrilling because I'm a lifelong horror fan, so this is a dream to see something I've created being embraced by people. I feel grateful, and the older I get, the more I appreciate it. I'm like, oh my God, I don't have to retire yet! It's just been the best thing. Also, with the longevity, it's been an interesting thing to do, to build on Chucky's story like a sandcastle over decades with the same people, also bringing in new people for a fresh perspective. Those I've worked with have really contributed to the success of the show.

The first Child's Play film was in 1988, and obviously no one could have predicted how much of an impact Chucky would have. Did Don have a feeling he was on to something special?

> I think because it was the '80s—and at this point I was a horror fan and fledgeling filmmaker starting

out in LA—I had been watching *Halloween* and *Friday the 13th, Nightmare on Elm Street,* all these wonderful franchises with iconic villains. So, that became my specific goal and dream, to create something like that. The fact that it came true was amazing. I worked with a lot of smart people who helped this to come together, and it just worked. I was excited; Kirschner showed me a cut of the first movie as it was being worked on in postproduction and going through edits. But as for Chucky himself, it was obvious that he was going to work as a character from the very beginning.

I have heard so many theories online about what Chucky as a character was inspired by. Some are very conflicting ideas, but what was true?

I have come across things online that are simply not true. I've read that Robert the Doll inspired him, and that's just not the case. I had never heard of that at the time. Nor was the look of Chucky meant to mimic My Buddy doll, even though in the initial script he was called Buddy. It was actually inspired by the Cabbage Patch Kid craze in the '80s. Those dolls were hugely popular; we even had riots with people trying to get hold of the dolls, like on those huge sales, like Black Friday or that kind of thing.

Retail was going crazy over them. I found it fascinating on a cultural level. People are getting upset over them and are desperate to buy one. These things were heavily marketed to children, and it gripped everyone, and I knew how cynical all that was, that these companies were referring to kids as "consumer trainees," wanting kids to buy stuff they don't actually need. There was something about it that really struck me. Chucky was a metaphor for that craze. After a while, though, the films changed and evolved, so in later films and the TV series, Chucky becomes an archetype and metaphor for many things in our culture.

Several movies into the franchise now, it's been fantastic to see how Chucky has evolved. Was it always clear to Don how he wanted to take things and what direction things would go, or had he taken things on a film-by-film basis?

I didn't look that far ahead at the beginning. And even the story of *Child's Play 2*, all we knew was we wanted Andy to come back. I wanted to have Andy's mother back in the film for the second, but it didn't happen. I don't know why to this day. But as the years went on, I had a notion of what I wanted to do. I knew it was evident that people liked the character of Tiffany. I wanted to use Jennifer Tilly bodily as well as in the doll. One of my favourite segments is the first half hour of *Bride of Chucky* because of Jennifer.

When Jennifer Tilly joined the Child's Play world, fans absolutely adored her character. Jennifer brought so much to the franchise. I asked Don what it was like to create her character and to work alongside Jennifer.

Absolutely, and they are a great team when they work together, Brad Dourif (Chucky) and Jennifer. They work so well on screen. When I wrote the character Tiffany, I wanted it to be Jennifer Tilly. It was her in my mind all along. I wanted a character and personality that was someone who could come up against Brad. She has a wonderful voice for a largely vocal performance, too, of course. I was always a big fan of Jennifer's, from way back, so I knew I wanted to work with her.

The Chucky TV series has really given the Child's Play world a whole new generation of fans and a new lease on life. Would there be another series? I was keen to know.

I honestly don't know, but I do hope so. Hollywood is in a very weird place right now (at the time of writing, 2024) since the strikes, and there's a lot of slowness. They haven't cancelled us; they're just trying to find the best way to make it work for them and us. Finding the right network is a big part of that, and they're trying to figure that out. I know I would like to do it, and I have the story ready and pitched. But at the same time, I am also working on another Chucky movie. So, no matter what happens, Chucky still has a future ahead of him.

With Chucky being so loved by horror fans, and the films and TV series having become such classics, I wanted to understand how Don dealt with the pressure that comes along with that.

I definitely feel pressure, certainly with the TV show because we had to do it in such quick succession. There's so many milestones in television, and getting renewed is the biggest one. So, when we got renewed for [season] two, I wondered, How could we beat that? How could we do better? Like, on Rotten Tomatoes we got [a] 91 percent rating, so how do we move forward with that? Those kinds of thoughts would torture me, but, ultimately, I just trusted the process, and [trusted that the premise] of the show resonates with people. My fellow writers, directors, and producers have all done a great job in making this work.

Chapter 6

David Kirschner and I would flatter ourselves by saying we were the broccoli of the horror genre [laughs]. I've always admired and loved the idea of working with the same people and becoming a family with those on the show.

Although Chucky is an evil villain, I know fans absolutely adore his character. I wanted to know if Don has a soft spot for him like the fans do.

Oh, definitely, absolutely! Chucky is hilarious. I love his sense of humour and his perspective on the world; it's so cynical and subversive. He's a good conduit for my sensibilities, I guess.

Being a bit of a legend in the horror world himself, I asked what Don's own favourite horror movies are.

I like the older ones, the ones that I grew up on and watched: *Carrie*, *Rosemary's Baby*, *The Omen*. I loved them. The first *Nightmare on Elm Street* was great too; it's such a cool concept. More recently, I loved *Hereditary*; it was brilliant. I really liked *Get Out*. So many great films out there. I thought the Insidious franchise was fun. I love haunted house stories, and I've been working on an idea for that myself. I love the haunted house as a concept and a horror metaphor;

it's fun and we are due [for] another. I hope I get to do one.

With all my time spent studying haunted dolls and objects, I just had to dig deeper and find out if Don believed if such a thing was possible.

I guess I'd have to call myself a sceptic but only because I have not personally experienced anything supernatural, which is frustrating because I'd love to. But I'm not dismissive of the notion of it. I always feel with things like this, with notions of an afterlife, none of that would ultimately be any more bizarre or miraculous than life itself, right? I think there's that little [sliver] of possibility for almost everyone. Even if you're an atheist, I'm sure so many carry some hope. Interestingly, Jennifer Tilly believes and has had experiences. There's been a couple of times when she has [rung] me after having a dream, and then what she describes actually ended up happening in my life. That's fascinating to me.

I am fascinated by dolls and the idea of dolls being haunted.

It is interesting. Just setting aside the supernatural ramifications, we have such a primal response to dolls. Dolls are distortions of the human form, and there's something subtly disturbing about that; that artificiality is disturbing on a primal level.

Interview with Actress Jennifer Tilly

Jennifer Tilly's name has become intertwined with the legend of Child's Play. Her character in the franchise, Tiffany, has become as loved and revered as Chucky himself, and it is not hard to see why. Feisty, charming, sexy, and scary all in one, Tiffany has it all, and has certainly made Chucky face his match. Jennifer has, since arriving in the franchise in the late '90s, made a big splash in the horror world and has added a fresh perspective to the scary doll trope.

I spoke with her over the phone, and we spent a solid hour talking about her role, her love of Tiffany, and why the Child's Play universe has appealed to so many of us. I began by asking her about the most recent *Chucky* television series.

> We had the pandemic with absolutely nothing going on, and all of a sudden, Don called me, and I was off to Toronto for five months to film the series. It was great. There's so many layers in the Chucky series. I'm proud to be part of it, especially as the main character is based on a young Don Mancini. It's like a coming-of-age story but tagged as a "coming of rage story."

With Tiffany having now been part of the Chucky universe for so long, I wondered what Jennifer found the toughest about the role of Tiffany. On screen it looks so easy, so natural, but of course, I understood that her job was to make it look so.

> Tiffany is an acting challenge for me because she never ages. I'm at this age of my life where it's usually all grannies [laughs], and yet Don wants me to be sexy and fabulous! She's such a fun character to play though, especially after the pandemic, getting to be glamorous and strut around again. It was so much fun.

I think about the sexiness and inclusiveness of the series. There is certainly a lot of sexuality and emotion to the project.

> It's ahead of its time. The goth girls and goth boys and lesbians, they've always loved the Chucky series because there [have] always been positive role models in it, and it's such an inclusive show. In *Seed of Chucky*, we have John Waters, a gay icon! The character Glen/Glenda, Chucky's child, many in the trans community have said they really embraced him as a character. But apparently in the Chucky

series, *Seed* was quite a reviled film, but I happened to love it because it was about me, ha!

I told Jennifer that I absolutely loved that film, and she readily agreed.

I loved *Seed of Chucky*! There are so many layers to my character. In the movie, I'm literally chasing around myself as a doll, being a fan of myself. It's so much fun. In that movie, Tiffany is living Jennifer's movie star life. There's a scene where she goes to an event as Jennifer. She loves being a movie star; she loves the glamour and adoration she gets. So in *Seed of Chucky*, it was fun to do their different voices: Tiffany has plastic doll lungs, so I make her sound more dolly. At times, I had a bit of a Marilyn Monroe voice.

I was intrigued by this. Did she often get to make suggestions about what happened to her story and character?

In *Seed of Chucky*, when I knew it was about me, I was so delighted, and we threw around ideas and jokes. I said I wanted him to make me the diva, a bitch actress from hell. "Jennifer Tilly is so mean," the studio said, and I think they wanted a sweet girl! We actually had to reshoot a scene: There's a scene where Jennifer discovers a dead body. She leaves the studio and is surrounded by paparazzi asking her about the body, and as she gets in the limo, I played it like she was really thrilled and feeling relevant again. She was happy to be all over the news! But we had to reshoot the scene; the studio said it makes Jennifer look too mean. So I redid the lines and had to make myself sound a bit more sympathetic. But yes, I helped write certain things and certain lines. You know that line in *Seed of Chucky* where Tiffany is dragging Jennifer's body? She says, "Fuck, she's fat!" I came up with that!

I certainly remember the scene and know fans all had a good laugh at the antics of Jennifer's character. Over time, though, I felt it was fair to say that Don Mancini took Chucky to a darker place again.

Yes. Don wanted to make Chucky scary again. Chucky had been around for so long, and he decided to get him back to his horror roots. "Let's make Chucky scary again," he said. So he put the whole *Seed of Chucky* thing aside and then made it all darker again with *Cult of Chucky*. I came in as a cameo. I didn't get much of an input in those last two movies, but Don always has a plan. Like when he brought back Andy Barclay. These things aren't a plotline; he's always thinking ahead about what he wants and who he wants.

Tiffany's character is explored quite deeply in the series, isn't she?

Yes. I'm semi-retired, so I'm just enjoying life, enjoying being with my boyfriend, and not having to work. So when he sent me the script, I was so happy, as he really went into Tiffany's backstory. It was amazing to see a younger actress playing me in the backstory scenes, and I realised how horrible [the character] is! I always tried to justify Tiffany's kills and her bad actions, but when I saw someone else playing her, I thought, She's not nice at all!

She is so diabolical and unhinged, which is so delicious to play.

I couldn't *not* ask Jennifer her opinion on why the Chucky franchise has become so popular. I wanted to know why, in her opinion, it became so loved.

Well, the doll is so adorable! As a Good Guy doll, he is so cute. And the doll in the series is amazing. When I watched the puppeteers working Chucky, he looked so sweet and innocent, yet he has Brad's nasty snarl. It's hypnotic. People really identify with

Chucky, too. They identify with him: He's a working guy with a nagging wife, a genderfluid kid, a midlife crisis, like in *Seed of Chucky*.

Also, Brad. Brad understands Chucky. He is doing Oscar-nominated acting in the movies. In the first film I did, *Bride of Chucky*, Brad and I went into the booth together to actually interact together rather than recording separately. In one scene, I felt such profound sadness, and he's giving me so much with his eyes, and I started to cry, and he started to cry. Brad is a lot of Chucky's appeal, I think. He's very powerful.

Plus, Don. He's a Chucky fan himself and a horror fan. So he's like a kid with candy! He thinks, What would I like to see? As a Chucky fan, what would I want to see? Which is why he brought back Andy Barclay. And the fans went wild! Alex is great; he loves doing it, and the fans go insane for him.

Tiffany is a big part of why fans love the show, though, right?

I hope so. Fans love her, and they dress up as her at Halloween. The fans are so creative. Sometimes they are a better Tiffany than me! And also, the kids who dress up as her, they do wonderful things. There's even a dog's outfit. Google it and trust me.

It's really funny; it makes the dog look like a Chucky running towards you!

The Great Gabbo (1929)

The '80s and '90s seemed to be *the* decade for the evil doll subgenre; however, the theme of creepy dolls goes as far back as the 1920s.

The Great Gabbo was a sound film—actually, one of the earliest examples of audio in motion picture after years of silent movies. A black-and-white production based on the short story "The Rival Dummy" by Ben Hecht, *The Great Gabbo* is certainly one of film history's earliest examples of using a doll as the catalyst for unsettling horror.

The movie follows central character Gabbo, who is a brilliant stage ventriloquist. As the story unfolds, we find that Gabbo is mentally unstable and mistreats his young assistant, blaming her for the lack of success he's having with his act. His assistant eventually quits; however, she soon finds herself working for Gabbo again. After he makes a romantic move on her, she rejects him, and thus begins a dark, psychologically uncomfortable journey using Gabbo's dummy as a catalyst for unfolding horror.

Dead of Night (1945)

Dead of Night is a black-and-white British anthology horror film, with the individual segments created by different directors. It was released to mostly positive reviews, particularly for the segment that I will be focusing on here.

The *Dead of Night* anthology has five different stories within the film: "The Hearse Driver," "The Christmas Party," "The Haunted Mirror," "The Golfer's Story," and "The Ventriloquist's Dummy."

It is "The Ventriloquist's Dummy" that I will be focusing on here, for obvious reasons. This segment of the creepy film follows central character Maxwell Frere, who runs a stage act using a ventriloquist dummy he calls Hugo. Using flashbacks as part of the storytelling, we learn that Hugo is a dummy who seems out of control and often insults guests and even his host, Frere. Hugo appears to be a vindictive and manipulative dummy with a life of his own—a possessed vessel. The film follows the unfolding drama between Frere and Hugo, with the eventual mental breakdown of Frere highlighted in the climax of the segment.

Devil Doll (1964)

Devil Doll is a British horror film that follows a troubled magician and ventriloquist, who is extremely popular in London after performing his stage show to packed-out theatres night after night. His dummy is called Hugo, and he is the central part of the act, playing an antagonistic character to his host.

An American journalist, keen to learn more about the act, brings his girlfriend, Marianne, to see the show with him, leading to a nightmare for the couple. It seems the infamous ventriloquist has a penchant for trapping souls in dolls … who will be next?

Trilogy of Terror (1975)

Trilogy of Terror is a horror anthology film from the '70s, and each story is written by respected author Richard Matheson. Actress Karen Black stars as the main character in each segment. The stories in the anthology are unrelated, each telling their own unique tale; however, it is the third in the film that explores the theme of a creepy doll, and it's called "Amelia."

Short film "Amelia" tells the story of central character Amelia who lives alone in an apartment. The film opens as she returns home from a shopping spree in which she has purchased a wooden doll, which she was told housed a spirit. The necklace the doll wears is said to keep the spirit trapped inside it. Amelia speaks to her mum over the phone, and an argument ensues. Hanging up, Amelia realises that the doll's necklace has somehow been broken and all hell breaks loose.

Magic (1978)

Magic is a horror film based on the novel by William Goldman. The unsettling movie received positive reviews from critics. *Magic* follows the story of failed magician Corky, who wants to find success as a stage act. After failed attempts, he returns with a new gimmick: his ventriloquist dummy who he calls Fats. Fats helps Corky make a huge name for himself, and he finally receives the success that he's been after. However, soon the film explores the psychological issues of Corky and how he eventually cannot control Fats, who has become an outlet for his dark side. Corky becomes a victim of his own ventriloquist doll in many ways as this alter ego begins to control him more and more.

Magic was directed by Richard Attenborough and stars Anthony Hopkins, Ann-Margret, and Burgess Meredith.

In 1978, Anthony Hopkins was interviewed by Bobbie Wygant about his time making the movie. He confirmed he had actually learned ventriloquism to do the role: "It's the art of misdirection … It looks like it's coming from the dummy's mouth, but in fact it's coming from here," he states, pointing to his mouth. He also said Fats the dummy used to make him laugh. "I used to get a kind of kick out of him … Some people were frightened of him."[35]

Many found the character of Corky quite a tragic one, including Hopkins. "The sad thing about Corky … is that he never grows up … In his adult body it makes him highly dangerous … He cannot face reality … He doesn't face reality at all. And he faces reality, confronts reality, through this doll called Fats."[36]

---

35. The Bobbie Wygant Archive, "Anthony Hopkins for 'Magic' 1978—Bobbie Wygant Archive," posted May 29, 2020, YouTube, 11 min., 52 sec., https://www.youtube.com/watch?v=jKNwF7tp64Y.

36. Bobbie Wygant Archive, "Anthony Hopkins."

Dolls (1987)

A year before the first *Child's Play* film landed, the film *Dolls* arrived. The seventy-seven-minute film has aged well, with a core of fans still rating it highly to this day. The film received mixed to generally positive reviews during its release. Much like *Dolly Dearest* and *Dead Silence*, the *Dolls* movie has not just one but an army of evil dolls.

Dolls tells the story of six people who are caught in a violent thunderstorm as they seek help and refuge. They approach a nearby mansion, where they are invited in by the couple who live there. Of course, this is a horror film, so things don't end too well. During their stay, the stranded people realise the house is inhabited by many dolls and toys, each of whom are alive and have a thirst for blood. The film shares the journey of the six inhabitants of the Gothic mansion as they fight for survival against the dolls that seem to have a merciless appetite for death and destruction.

Pin (1988)

Pin is an '80s Canadian horror film, and it's based on the novel of the same name, which was authored by Andrew Neiderman in 1981.

Described by some as an unsettling psychological thriller, *Pin* follows the Linden family. Dysfunctional and troubled, the two children look to their parents for guidance. Their father, Dr. Frank Linden, has a life-size dummy which he uses to communicate valuable lessons to his offspring. However, outside of his discussions with the children using the dummy, he is a cold and distant father. The children soon take to treating the dummy like a brother, to unsettling and unnerving results.

The Puppet Master Series (1989)

The Puppet Master series is an American film franchise and has become one of the longest-running film series in the genre. Not all evil, the puppets who have come to life in this production are an unusual mix: some are good, some are bad, some are antiheroes.

The first film was intended for cinematic release; however, it was released straight to VHS. The film became a cult success, and fans have followed the creepy toy drama from the '80s up until the present day. The Puppet Master series tells the story of a group of puppets which have been brought to life, and each one has a unique power and ability.

The first film in the series shows the central character being plagued by unsettling visions. He and several other psychics visit the Bodega Bay Inn, where they discover that one of their friends has taken his own life. As the visions evolve and continue to happen, the group starts to understand that something sinister is occuring. Soon, they find themselves hunted by a group of killer dolls that have been created by a twisted puppeteer called Andre Toulon.

There have been over fourteen Puppet Master films (at the time of publication), and each story uses the animated puppets as a catalyst for the unfolding drama. Whilst some films are interconnected (with several being viewed as prologues or spin-offs), the stories are interlinked by the puppets themselves.

Other films in the series include *Curse of the Puppet Master* and *Puppet Master vs. Demonic Toys*.

Dolly Dearest (1991)

Dolly Dearest is an independent American supernatural horror film. Hot off the heels of *Child's Play* in 1988, *Dolly Dearest* landed on screen—this time with a female doll of an evil persuasion. The doll in this film is known only by the name "Dolly" and is a cute porcelain creation with long dark hair and a velvet red dress. However, as the film continues, her face contorts and becomes much more sinister looking.

The movie follows character Sam Elliot as he and his family move to Mexico, where he has taken ownership of a doll manufacturing factory. Things seem to be going great for the family as they settle into their new lives in Mexico. However, soon Sam's daughter begins to act strangely as she develops an obsession with one doll in particular. This doll, as I'm sure you can guess if you haven't already seen the film, proceeds to wreak havoc on the lives of the family, as they have unwittingly unleashed an evil presence in the area.

May (2002)

May is a psychological horror film, and it's admittedly a bit of a different style of entry in this book. Whilst the term "doll" is used to describe the movie, it is not in the traditional sense.

Upon its release, *May* was unfortunately not a success at the box office; however, it received positive reviews from critics and has had a cult following ever since.

The film follows central character May. May had a troubling childhood: She was an outcast at school and had a difficult upbringing, leading her to a disturbed and insecure life as a young adult woman. She finds it difficult to make and maintain friendships, leaving her continually isolated. It is this backdrop of loneliness that lends May a hand in pulling her into a deep web of increasingly disturbed behaviour. The movie portrays May's descent into madness, and a life-size doll becomes the catalyst for the story's unfolding horror.

Saw Franchise (2004–)

In total, there are an impressive nine Saw movies in the popular American horror franchise (with a tenth being planned at the time of writing). Violent and often extremely gory, the Saw films have been going since the early 2000s. They began after Leigh Whannell and James Wan pitched the concept to movie companies by sharing with them their short film of the same name. The short film was used as a selling point to potential film companies, made allegedly on a budget of only $5,000.

The Saw franchise follows the trail of a demented serial killer known as Jigsaw, who tortures his victims in unsettling ways if he believes they are guilty of a crime or lacking in appreciation for their life and time on earth. Where Jigsaw is different, though, is that he doesn't kill people directly. He sets up mazes, games, and challenges that the victims have to work their way through for a chance to survive.

So, where does the doll come in? Known as Billy the Puppet, this creepy-looking doll is used as the device in which messages are sent from the killer to his victims during their fight for survival.

The Doll Master (2004)

The Doll Master is a South Korean movie that, like several other films we have explored, doesn't have just one creepy doll, but a whole host of them. This film ranks high on the scare factor and is one of the best offerings from Korea in the horror genre.

The Doll Master follows five central characters, each of whom have been invited to stay at a retreat. The retreat also houses many dolls, which are all delicately handmade by the woman who owns the building in which they are all staying.

After a time, several of the characters are killed, and it soon becomes apparent that the dolls on the property are inhabited by spirits who are out for revenge. The question is, why?

Dead Silence (2007)

A film about a scary doll is good enough for most of us horror fans, but some films have a whole host of scary dolls in waiting.

Dead Silence is about characters Jamie and his wife, Lisa, after they receive an unusual and creepy-looking ventriloquist doll in the post. However, they don't know who sent it. Shortly after the doll arrives, Lisa is found dead, and so begins Jamie's journey to uncovering where the doll came from and how it links to his wife's grizzly demise.

The story follows Jamie as he returns to the town in which he grew up, Ravens Fair, where he learns about the famous ventriloquist Mary Shaw. Jamie soon discovers that there are many hidden secrets in his old hometown (with many dolls out for vengeance).

The film begins with one creepy doll, Billy, but soon the film includes a cast of creepy ventriloquist dolls. *Dead Silence* was often overlooked at the time of release, but since, it has gained quite the following. There are even *Dead Silence* dolls available on the market, which have become highly collectible.

Dead Silence was directed by James Wan and written by Leigh Wannell, who were both involved in the *Saw* franchise.

James Wan is an Australian producer, director, and screen-writer. In recent years, he has become a legend of the horror industry, with his name behind iconic movies such as the Insidious series, the Conjuring universe, the Saw franchise, *Lights Out*, and *Malignant*.

The Doll in the Dark (2011)

The Doll in the Dark, which is also known in some territories as *The Melancholy Fantastic*, is quite an obscure indie hor-ror produced in America. It first found an audience through being played at various popular film festivals. While the film explores very dark and creepy themes, it isn't strictly horror.

The Doll in the Dark explores the life of a young girl, called Melanie Crow, who is suffering with grief after the loss of her mother to suicide. Troubled and low, she searches for a way to find some comfort and company. In a twisted and creepy turn of events, Melanie Crow decides to create a life-size doll to keep her company. However, soon the doll begins to impart messages to the girl, and most of them are fright-ening in nature.

I was both moved and unnerved by the film and wanted to find out more. I invited A. D. Calvo, the director, to dis-cuss his work on *The Melancholy Fantastic*.

Interview with Director A. D. Calvo
This is such a powerful film about death and grief, so it felt natural to begin the interview by talking about these themes and what inspired the movie.

> I had just come off of a cancelled feature project that collapsed right after the October 2008 financial crisis. So it was a year's worth of effort down the drain.

It was then that he turned his focus elsewhere—a movie about a doll. But ultimately, it was so much more. The doll in the film represents the central character's grief in many ways.

> I wanted the doll to be a central character, so the look of the thing was key. I searched high and low and eventually bought an antique bisque doll on eBay. I then had a talented friend sculpt a life-size mask of it. And my wife, a decent seamstress, created the muslin body, which we aged with tea.

I know I found the doll quite unsettling to look at. I told A. D. this, and he agreed it was certainly creepy.

> It was a bit eerie whenever the camera panned over to it; it took on a life of its own. I keep the original on a shelf in a hallway, and that hallway always feels haunted.

Though the doll took centre stage in the unfolding horror, the actress's performance really shone. I put this to A. D.

Definitely. She was a stand-in on an earlier film, and whenever the camera was on her, we all took notice. She was supernatural in front of the camera and very easy-going and took direction well, so I wrote it with her in mind.

With there being so many doll-themed horror movies out there, I wondered what inspired this project. Were *Child's Play* and *Annabelle* influences at all?

Not so much of those, specifically. However, at least initially, the film was compared to *May* (which I liked) and *Pin* (which I hadn't yet seen). But if there's any influence, it would probably be *Magic* (1978). I find mannequins creepy, so this is more of a crossover between the doll and mannequin niche.

The Robert Franchise (2015–2019)

If you have read this far, then you'll know about the true-life account of Robert the Doll, who is said to be haunted. He currently resides in Florida's Fort East Martello Museum, where he is carefully locked away behind a glass cabinet to stop any potential damage he may want to unleash upon visitors. However, due to his infamy, Robert has inspired countless articles, books, and now a movie franchise by British indie director Andrew Jones. Robert the Doll was designed and created by artist Susan Mitchell.

Jones, a prolific screenwriter and director of several horror titles, including *The Last House On Cemetery Lane* and *The Exorcism of Anna Ecklund*, released the first of four films about Robert the Doll in 2015. Although Jones was inspired by the true-life accounts of the doll, he also added his own imagination into the mix and went on to make *The Revenge of Robert the Doll*, *The Curse of Robert the Doll*, *The Toymaker*, and *Robert Reborn*.

Robert tells the story of how a maid gave the family she worked for the doll as a gift. The parents in turn give the doll to their son, Gene, to play with. It soon becomes apparent that the doll is possessed by a dangerous entity who not only plays cruel tricks on the family, but also gets involved in the torture and murder of those who get in his way.

The other films in Jones's franchise are not based on the urban legend of the real Robert the Doll; instead, they are expansions of the story based on the director's imaginings.

Interview with Director Andrew Jones

There are so many horror films out there, but I was curious as to why Andrew felt moved to make a film about the Robert legend.

When *Annabelle* became a hit film in 2014, our distribution [partner] 4Digital Media were shopping around for other real-life haunted doll stories. I discussed it with the team there, and we settled on Robert the Doll as the most intriguing of the stories, and our investors agreed to finance the film. It should have been a period piece, but we only had a miniscule budget for the first film, so we had to set it in the modern era.

With films like *Child's Play* and *Annabelle* out there, I wondered if Andrew was a big fan of the killer doll subgenre himself. Presumably he had a love of the theme?

Very much so. I love the Chucky series and other lesser-known gems like *Dolly Dearest* and *Pinocchio's Revenge*, also the Puppet Master franchise of course, which we paid homage to in later entries in the Robert series.

It's known that the Robert franchise was filmed on a limited budget, so I was curious what challenges this presented to Andrew and his team.

We couldn't afford the kind of technology films like *Child's Play* had, so puppeteering the doll is always the biggest challenge. You can't pull off many full-body shots so have to break the coverage down and shoot only the doll's legs, face, or upper torso in close-ups. It becomes time consuming, but as a low-budget exploitation filmmaker, you have to do the best you can with the limitations you're presented with.

Did the budget create limitations with the shooting schedule?

As with most of our early films, we had an eight-day shooting schedule, which is obviously a very short amount of time to complete a feature! Money is always a challenge, but time is the really stressful factor when making these low-budget movies. We kept locations to a minimum, shooting mainly in one house, but it's still a tall order to shoot everything in a week. You always feel like you emerge with a film which isn't as complete as it could have been if you'd had a few extra days.

Fans have since come to love the Robert franchise, but was Andrew himself pleased with the result?

I thought there were some great scenes but not a great overall film. When I look back, I can see the sequences we had the time on and others which suffered from not having enough time. But it was a profitable venture for our business partners, hence why we made four other Robert films after the first.

The doll in the film looks nothing like the Robert of the supernatural legend. I wanted to know what inspired his appearance.

An artist actually drew Robert's facial design, and to this day, he wants to remain uncredited, as he works for a big company and did it on the side as a favour. Susan then created the head in America, and we had it shipped to the UK. My wife, Sharron, created the costume.

Much like Annabelle, the film version of Robert has a very different look to the real-life doll, purely because the distributors wanted him to look creepier.

Several Robert films are under Andrew's belt, and fans would love to know if there might be more to come.

The films have been successful business ventures for the distributors and investors, so there may be more in the future. I would only be involved if we can come up with a fresh take. I think it would need to have some kind of new angle with new characters to give it a shot at finding a wider audience. But even if there are no more films made, the series does have a small cult following, which I'm very grateful for.

Interview with Susan Mitchell, the Doll Artist Behind Robert

The doll from the Robert movies is a work of art, and looking at him with his intricate detail I wondered how long the artist had spent developing her skill.

I've been making dolls for over twenty years now.

I had read that Andrew Jones, the director, knew how he wanted Robert to look, but was it true, and how did the doll measure up to expectations?

It was all Andrew's idea, how Robert should look. He sent me a very detailed artist's illustration, which I used as a reference picture. I only made Robert's head, and I think it took a little over a month, just because I was waiting for the supplies to be shipped. The biggest challenge was making his eyes. I used glass eyes from a taxidermy supply company and asked them if I could paint the eyes and they said no. But I tried anyway with heat-set paint, and it worked just fine.

With the artist's many years of experience, I was interested to know if she had created dolls for other projects.

I made a postmortem doll for a customer from France that was making a film about the drug Krokodil and just recently made a doll for an independent filmmaker in North Carolina that wanted a doll that resembled a puppet from the Mr. Rogers TV show.

Robert fans were impressed with the appearance of the doll, but how did Susan feel about seeing him on screen?

I got a kick out of seeing Robert look so menacing!

The Annabelle Franchise (2014–2019)

Ed and Lorraine Warren, the famous paranormal investigators and demonologists, were the ones who brought the infamous story of the evil Annabelle doll to light. Annabelle's legendary story made a huge mark on the field of paranormal study and an equally big impact on the film world. Although the real Annabelle doll is housed in the Warrens' Occult Museum in Connecticut, the now-famous Annabelle doll of the subsequent film franchise is in the hands of movie fans the world over as a collectible toy.

Annabelle (2014)

The *Annabelle* film is said to be based on the account told by the Warrens in the '70s—but with obvious dramatic enhancements. It begins with three student nurses who have called in the Warrens for help after a doll in their apartment began moving different places than where they'd left it. The film itself veers off from what the Warrens said happened, but the movie is a tense, creepy journey from start to finish.

Annabelle the Doll in the film franchise is a tall, vintage girl in a white dress, with large, bulging eyes—very different to the "real" Annabelle that was a Raggedy Ann doll.

Annabelle makes a fascinating villain in the film. Unlike in the Child's Play movies, this doll doesn't speak or physically move—the negative energy is attached and all around the doll, so the audience sees things happen but by unseen hands.

Annabelle: Creation (2017)

Annabelle: Creation is the second installment of the series about the infamous doll. The story follows middle-aged couple Samuel and Esther, who, after the tragic loss of their daughter, try to embed her soul into one of the dolls that Samuel has created.

Unbeknownst to them, the spirit now trapped inside the doll isn't their daughter at all, but an insatiable demon who is behind a series of terrifying events.

Gary Dauberman, an American screenwriter and director, is behind *Annabelle: Creation* and *Annabelle Comes Home*. He is also the writer behind *The Nun* and *It: Chapter Two*, amongst many others.

Annabelle Comes Home (2019)

Central character Judy is the young daughter of the Warrens. In this third instalment of the Annabelle franchise, we visit Judy at home as she is being cared for by a teenage babysitter. During the babysitter's weekend looking after Judy, the Annabelle doll is disturbed and unwittingly unleashed by a guest, and the evil truly begins…

The Doll Factory (2014)

The Doll Factory is a grindhouse horror, and much like some of the later films in the Child's Play franchise, there is a sprinkling of black comedy throughout, giving the movie some lighter, fun moments.

Set in the 1970s, *The Doll Factory* follows a group of teens as they decide to leave a Halloween party in favour of heading to a local house that's said to be haunted. Armed with a book of spells and eager for some spooky fun, the friends head into the property and cast a spell, which has the effect of bringing the many dolls inside to life. Then the horror truly begins!

The Boy (2016)

The Boy focuses on the character Greta Evans. She has moved from America to the UK to escape her numerous personal troubles. She has been hired to be a nanny to a couple's son at their large estate. However, once Greta arrives and is introduced to Brahms, she is shocked to see he is not a real boy, but instead a large doll. The doll is treated like a human being by the couple, who then give Greta a list of rules on how they want her to take care of the doll in their absence.

In 2020, William Brent Bell released *Brahms: The Boy II*, a stand-alone film. Although the film featured the very same doll, the acting cast were different, and the storyline veered into different territory. Bell has also worked on numerous other horror films since his career began.

The Doll (2016)

The Doll is an Indonesian horror film and was released in 2016, with the sequel following in 2017. The movie centres on the creepy events that happen to a young couple, Daniel and Anya, after Daniel finds a doll in the project site where he's been working. Thinking his partner will like it, he brings the doll home. Anya is happy to keep the toy until she realises that frightening events seem to follow in its wake. Anya looks into the history of the doll and its association with death and murder. Like in most doll-themed horror films, this doll simply won't stay still and roams about causing turmoil and trouble.

The Doll 2 (2017) uses a different doll; however, it is considered a sequel to the first movie. The plot revolves around a mother who uses the doll to communicate with her dead daughter.

The Doll Master (2017)

The Doll Master, directed by Steven M. Smith, tells the tale of Norman, a mentally unstable young man who spends all his free time with a doll called Hugo. Norman and Hugo share everything, including meals, movies, and even conversation. The plot turns darker when the doll goes missing, sending Norman on a desperate journey to uncover where his friend is. Along the way, he becomes involved with a reality TV show, which exploits his unstable and vulnerable nature.

Sabrina (2018)

Sabrina is an Indonesian horror film. It was directed by Rocky Soyaya, who also directed the Indonesian film *The Doll* from the entry above.

The unsettling (English subtitled) release, which at the time of writing is only available on super-streaming service Netflix, is fast becoming a popular gem within the horror community, especially with the creepy doll as its main focus.

Sabrina explores the story of a man and his wife who run a toy manufacturing company. They have adopted a young girl, Vanya, and in her honour have created a special edition doll just for her. However, Vanya is troubled after recently losing her mother, and in a bid to contact her mother from the other side, takes part in the paranormal Charlie Charlie challenge. Things go wrong, however, and soon a demon is unleashed, wreaking havoc on the family.

Child's Play (2019)

Child's Play is a reimagining of the original Chucky franchise, landing somewhere between a remake and a reboot. Following the loose narrative of the original *Child's Play*, this later film follows character Andy who is given the gift of a doll for his birthday by his mother. As is the same creepy problem in the original, Chucky comes to life and starts wreaking havoc and destruction; however, the "causes" aren't quite the same as in the original … the evil takes a very different route.

This version of *Child's Play* was directed by Lars Klevberg, and starred Aubrey Plaza, Gabriel Bateman, and Mark Hamill.

M3GAN (2022)

M3GAN is a sci-fi/horror film that follows eight-year-old girl Cady, who is sent to live with her aunt Gemma after her parents are killed in an accident. Gemma is a whizz at technology and is working on developing a robotic doll companion for kids. Eventually, Cady gets hold of the prototype of the M3GAN doll and brings it home, and she starts a friendship with the AI model.

Things go from bad to worse when M3GAN develops a mind of her own and dark and twisted things begin happening to those around her.

Longlegs (2024)

Longlegs is a psychological horror film starring Nicolas Cage and Maika Monroe. Directed and written by Osgood Perkins, the film received a positive response on Rotten Tomatoes.

Longlegs is a tense, psychological horror which follows the trail of central character FBI Agent Harker. An agent with psychic abilities, Harker is hired to try to solve the case of a serial killer known as Longlegs. Whilst the premise of the film certainly sounds like a detective mystery, there are plenty of supernatural twists and turns, including a deep dip into the occult. The film, whilst not about dolls in itself, explores Longlegs's character, who is a doll maker and who uses his dolls to execute his occult methods. The use of the dolls in *Longlegs* is exceptionally creepy and certainly warrants its inclusion in this volume.

Dolls in Film: In Conclusion

Exploring the history of film when it comes to the haunted and killer doll genre has been eye-opening, because it serves as a reminder that dolls are deeply embedded in our entertainment culture. We as humans appear to have a primal fear of these toys, and films tap into this by bringing the horror to life in the most literal and visceral ways. Whether it's Chucky, Annabelle, or any of the other scary dolls on screen that we've explored, the sheer number of movies that feature scary dolls highlights how we feel about these innocent-looking playthings.

CHAPTER 7
DOLLS IN LITERATURE

I have been a self-confessed book addict since childhood. In fact, I think my love of ghost stories and all things macabre was born at the age of nine when I began reading the Point Horror book series, which was aimed at older kids and teens. From then on, it was rare that you'd find me without a book in hand. I loved them, whether fiction or nonfiction. As long as they were creepy and full of horror and ghosts, I was all in.

As far as I am concerned, there's few better things in life than settling down in a cosy chair and delving into a scary book. Whilst movies can convey fear explicitly with sound effects, tense music, and on-screen violence, books are an altogether more subtle road to fear.

For this section, I have compiled a list of books which use the haunted or cursed doll theme as part of the central storyline. From the 1980s classics by Ruby Jean Jensen to modern publications from the likes of Ellen Datlow, here are some books you may want to check out.

The Dollhouse Murders by Betty Ren Wright (1983)

Betty Ren Wright was an American writer of numerous children's novels, many of which had unsettling, creepy themes. Her novels included *A Ghost in the Window* and *Ghosts Beneath Our Feet*.

The Dollhouse Murders is an eerie tale about a young girl called Amy, whose once-tranquil life soon turns into something terrifying when she realises the dolls and dollhouse she plays with in the attic are not just toys. She begins to suspect there is more to them when she visits the attic to find the dolls have moved about to different positions, and the lights of the dollhouse are on when they should be off. Amy believes there's something going on, but what? This is a chilling tale that'll put you off playing with dolls.

Ruby Jean Jensen

Ruby Jean Jensen was an American author of pulp horror fiction. Her titles often focused on creepy children, so it wasn't much of a surprise when she used dolls as a central theme in her work. Jensen had over twenty novels published and two hundred short stories. It is the following stories that contain dolls of darkness.

Mama (1983)

After her dad passed away, Dorrie found herself alone and scared. Not long after, she discovers a doll in the attic. Could this be the little friend she has been desperate for? Dorrie is delighted with the find, and soon she is attached to the mysterious doll. This isn't just an innocent plaything, though, and events soon take a turn for the worse...

Annabelle (1987)

Jessica, a five-year-old, lives a lonely and isolated life with a family who largely ignores her and a mother who walked out on her. Feeling the deep impact of her loneliness, she tries to find solace elsewhere.

Jessica finds a bundle of old, forgotten dolls lying in an abandoned house nearby and quickly finds herself emotionally attached to them. The housekeeper notices and is worried, but the family largely disregards her concerns.

Soon after, Jessica begins to experience a host of terrifying nightmares that seem to be linked, somehow, to the dolls which she has become so fond of. With the family around her in turmoil and Jessica increasingly frightened and alone, she sticks to the friends she has made: the dolls. But what is the truth about them? A family drama and a whole host of creepy dolls, this release is sure to unnerve readers.

Baby Dolly (1991)

Baby Dolly tells the story of a cursed doll and how it plagued one family through generations. Sybil received the baby doll when she was younger but had a bad feeling about it. There was just something she felt around the doll she could not explain, but what?

Not long after getting the doll, her sister passed away. The doll is placed in the attic and left to gather dust, but years later, her daughter, Rose, has a baby. Sybil gets the old doll down from the attic and gives it to the newborn. Soon after, the baby dies. A dark and creepy energy is attached to the doll…

Among the Dolls by William Sleator (1975)

William Sleator was an American novelist who produced more than thirty novels in his lifetime. His book *House of Stairs* is considered one of the best books of the twentieth century.

Among the Dolls follows Vicky, who is very disappointed. She wanted a new bike for her birthday, but instead, she has received a dollhouse. It isn't long, though, before she becomes enchanted by the small world and its inhabitants. With a difficult home life, Vicky begins to find her escape in the world of the dollhouse and soon starts to take out her anger and frustration on her dolls. It feels like a terrifying nightmare when Vicky wakes up inside the dollhouse one morning, and finds herself trapped with the dolls. *Among the Dolls* is a surreal tale that feels like a nightmare come true.

The Doll by Josh Webster (1986)

Josh Webster is the author of several horror and thriller titles of the '70s and '80s, including *Ceremonies*, *Quarantine*, and *The Beckoning*.

Gretchen and Mary are twins, and they are the central focus of *The Doll* by Webster. These twins look so much alike that it would be hard to tell thesm apart—but what does help tell them apart is the doll that Gretchen carries around with her every day, almost obsessively. She won't put the toy down. The doll, rather creepily, even looks a lot like the twin girls.

The doll soon takes on a force of its own, and Gretchen soon finds herself hearing it whisper to her…it utters terrible, nightmarish things. Will she listen?

Dolly: A Ghost Story by Susan Hill (2012)

Susan Hill has been a legend of the literary world since the release of her classic ghost story, *The Woman in Black* (1983). It went on to become a successful film (starring Daniel Radcliffe) and a legendary West End stage production.

Hill has always been the queen of creepy when it comes to literature, and her book *Dolly: A Ghost Story* is no exception. Set in the English Fens, the book follows young Edward, who is sent to stay with his aunt after the passing of his parents. His cousin, Leonora, is there too as well as a distant housekeeper. It soon becomes evident that Leonora is an unkind and bitter child, making Edward's stay at the foreboding location even more miserable.

It is after the gift of a dolly on her birthday that things take a dark and sinister turn in the remote household. Partly a ghost story and partly a coming-of-age tale, this creepy release from Susan Hill is well worth delving into. The story isn't a long one, but there's enough tension wedged between the pages for fans of the macabre to enjoy.

The Doll Collection Edited by Ellen Datlow (2015)

Ellen Datlow is an American science fiction and horror editor who has won several literary awards for her titles. She was the editor of *The Doll Collection*, which is a selection of short stories based on the creepy doll trope.

The Doll Collection is a collection of short stories that are, as expected, centred on the theme of dolls, and whilst the dolls contained within the volume are not evil, they are certainly spooky and unnerving. The collection includes a ventriloquist dummy, a fortune-telling doll, a figurine, and many more. The dolls are, of course, central to each of the stories and take readers on a disquieting journey.

The book contains stories by authors Joyce Carol Oates, Seanan McGuire, Carrie Vaughn, Pat Cadigan, Tim Lebbon, Richard Kadrey, Genevieve Valentine, and Jeffrey Ford. The collection includes doll photographs taken by Datlow amongst photos by other artists.

The House of Small Shadows by Adam Nevill (2014)

Adam Nevill is a British horror and fantasy author. He has released several successful titles, including *Apartment 16, No One Gets Out Alive,* and *The Ritual.* It was his novel *House of Small Shadows* which used creepy dolls, puppets, and preserved animals as a major aspect of the plot, and his fans loved it.

The character Catherine lies at the heart of this scary tale. *House of Small Shadows* follows her after the loss of her job. She is desperate to start afresh, so when she is offered the chance to catalogue the late M. H. Mason's creepy collection of antique dolls and puppets, she accepts.

In the new job, Catherine soon finds herself gaining access to Mason's entire collection of unusual pieces. It is when his niece joins Catherine at the property that she learns the dark and creepy meaning behind Mason's art. She tries to get on with her role, but sinister events begin to take hold.

A creepy and compelling tale, *House of Small Shadows* has it all: tension, dolls, creepy antiques, and family drama.

Frozen Charlotte by Alex Bell (2016)

Alex Bell is a British author who has released several paranormal titles in young adult and adult fiction. Her titles include *The Haunting, A Most Peculiar Toy Factory,* and *Jasmyn.* It is her books *Frozen Charlotte* and *Charlotte Says* that use dolls as a catalyst for supernatural horror.

Frozen Charlotte takes readers to Dunvegan School, a building that has been closed for many years. It has recently been purchased and renovated, so central character Sophie sees this as a chance to spend time with her relatives, who are now living there. The place is full of surprises for Sophie, as she spends long weeks exploring the vast property, but most unnerving of all is the room she discovers, which is full of dolls—and the ghost that seems to be living there.

Charlotte Says by Alex Bell (2017)

A prequel to *Frozen Charlotte*, this novel follows central character Jemima who has accepted a job at a school in the Isle of Skye. Things seem to be going well for her until she unexpectedly receives a box of Frozen Charlotte dolls. It is after receiving these creepy figurines that she suddenly begins to remember things that she'd rather forget…a séance involving dolls, a fight with her stepdad, and a fire that destroyed their home.

Soon, several terrible and terrifying occurrences unfold at the girls' school, and Jemima realises the Frozen Charlotte dolls are somehow connected.

The Doll's Eye by Marina Cohen (2017)

Marina Cohen is the author of several children's and young adult novels, including *The Inn Between* and *A Box of Bones*. She has a master's degree in French literature and has harboured a fascination for all things spooky since she was a child.

The Doll's Eye follows central character Hadley, who wishes she could turn back time and recapture life the way it once was. She now has to share her mother's attention with her new stepfamily, and they have moved to a house in the middle of nowhere. It seems, for Hadley, that nothing has changed for the better.

Hadley, in her loneliness, spends time exploring her new home and the surrounding land. One day, she discovers a doll's house and a collection of dolls, and this soon leads her into a truly twisted adventure. A creepy and haunting tale, perfect for younger readers.

The Curse of Doll Island by Ocean (2018)

Author Ocean is the writer behind several novels, including *Diary from Hell's Waiting Room* and *Love You Like a Woman*.

The Curse of Doll Island is a creepy and twisted story that takes us back hundreds of years ago, where we learn that a shaman has performed a curse. His actions have trapped the souls of two women into dolls, which are then left abandoned on an island. Many years later, we meet central character Rosie, who decides she needs to take a vacation. Whilst on her break, she meets a cute girl named Devin. Neither Rosie nor Devin believe the stories about how the dolls on the island they are vacationing on actually come alive when the sun sets at night. Yet they both soon learn that truth is stranger than fiction…

The Dollhouse Family by Mike Carey (2020)

Mike Carey, also known as M. R. Carey, is a British author of several novels, comics, and films. He penned the much-loved title *The Girl with All the Gifts* as well as its later film adaptation.

The Dollhouse Family follows central character Alice, a young girl who has just received a beautiful antique dollhouse, which contains a family of intricate dolls. The dollhouse grips Alice from the start, and it isn't long before the toy becomes her entire world. With an unexpected, magic twist, Alice realises she can enter the dollhouse and visit the family of dolls herself.

With Alice's own family life full of troubles, she is soon faced with a chance to change things. Can the dolls that live in the dollhouse grant her wishes, and if they can, at what price?

Dolls in Fiction: In Conclusion

The above books all cling to the idea of dolls being much more than innocent toys. Whilst any object may have the potential to be haunted, or to frighten us, there's just *something* about dolls … These small, human replicas hold much more than we may give them credit for. If the titles in this section show us anything, it is that we, as a society, actively look for the horror behind these toys, because we somehow sense there is something more to them. Dolls aren't just playthings, after all. Many of us sense this, and I suspect there is a reason why.

CONCLUSION

This book was years in the making; I spent so much of my time reading and researching haunted dolls *before* I even set pen to paper. Having lived and breathed the topic for so long, I can honestly say I feel deeply connected to the subject. I do believe haunted dolls exist; I think dolls can be haunted as much as any building. If a person's soul or energy can enjoy walking around certain rooms or buildings after death, then why would they not also choose to remain close to a beloved object? I don't necessarily believe it's common, but after all of my research, I do believe it happens.

Much like all aspects of the paranormal, so much remains a mystery. We live in a world where we want answers; we want to read the small print, see the truth in black and white. If there is anything I have learned from writing this book, it's that we will likely never have concrete answers regarding how such paranormal occurrences actually happen. But understanding the hows and whys does not undo the simple truth that many thousands of people across the world have experienced the reality of haunted objects. Their deeply personal and touching experiences are a testament in themselves to the fact that this world is full of much more than we will ever grasp.

I hope you enjoyed coming on this haunted doll exploration with me. Whether it was Peggy, Robert, Harold, or any of the other accounts within, I sincerely wish at least one of these characters struck a chord with you. Their stories, much like our own, need to be heard.

ACKNOWLEDGMENTS

I'd love to thank the many people who agreed to contribute their time and effort into making this project what it is. There are so many of you, but you know who you are.

A huge appreciation to all those who agreed to be interviewed for this book or who shared their personal experiences with me.

Special thanks goes to Rob from the *How Haunted? Podcast*.

A massive thanks goes to the team at Llewellyn for their belief and support in this project.

During the completion of this book, my friend Keith Chawgo sadly passed away. Keith's warmth, support, and humour are qualities I will always remember. In particular, I will always treasure the way he believed in my writing and cheered me on. Thank you, Keith.

BIBLIOGRAPHY

Auer, Cynthia. "Charley the Haunted Doll." Atlas Obscura. September 17, 2018. https://www.atlasobscura.com /places/charley-the-haunted-doll.

Baird, Roger. "World's Oldest Toy Unearthed in Siberian Grave of Bronze Age Child Buried 4,500 Years Ago." International Business Times. December 29, 2017. https://www.ibtimes.co.uk/worlds-oldest-to-unearthed -siberian-grave-bronze-age-child-buried-4500-years-ago -1653109.

Belasco, Jessica. "Story of Haunted Box Isn't Just a Tale Dreamed Up in Hollywood." *San Antonio News*. Updated September 21, 2012. https://www.mysanantonio.com /news/local/article/story-of-haunted-box-isn-t-just-a -tale-dreamed-up-3882396.php.

The Bobbie Wygant Archive. "Anthony Hopkins for 'Magic' 1978—Bobbie Wygant Archive." Posted May 29, 2020.

YouTube, 11 min., 52 sec. https://www.youtube.com /watch?v=jKNwF7tp64Y.

Busch, Caitlin. "'If They Don't Let Us Play, They All Go Away': Haunted Dolls That Would Scare Even Chucky." USA. August 23, 2022. https://www.usanetwork.com /usa-insider/scary-haunted-dolls-chucky.

David, Lauren. "La Pascualita: Bridal Shop Mannequin or Embalmed Corpse?" How Stuff Works. Updated May 17, 2024. https://people.howstuffworks.com/la-pascualita .htm.

ghostrekk. "Top 5 Most Haunted Dolls!!" Ghostrekk. February 17, 2016. https://ghostrekk.wordpress.com/2016 /02/17/top-5-most-haunted-dolls/.

Gornstein, Leslie. "A Jinx in a Box?" *Los Angeles Times*. July 25, 2004. https://www.latimes.com/la-ca-urban-legend -jewish-scroll-cabinet-t-20040725-story.html.

Grey, Orrin. "What's That in the Window? The Creepy Legend of the Janesville Doll." The Lineup. June 28, 2016. https://the-line-up.com/janesville-doll.

Hall, Ashley. "Joliet—The Doll with a Haunting Curse." The Paranormal Guide. February 14, 2013. http:// www.theparanormalguide.com/blog/joliet-the-doll -with-a-haunting-curse.

"Harold the Haunted Doll—An Infamous Case of the Paranormal." The Haunted Attic, accessed April 15, 2025, https://thehauntedattic.uk/2015/10/18/harold-the -haunted-doll-an-infamous-case-of-the-paranormal/.

Harris, Jayne. *Peggy the Doll: A Very Different Haunting.* Published by the author, 2017.

Harris, Meghan. "Mystery Surrounds 200-Year-Old 'Haunted Doll from Hell.'" *The Courier Mail.* October 11, 2016. https://www.couriermail.com.au/news/mystery -surrounds-200yearold-haunted-doll-from-hell /news-story/cdad1e331f15302212100f930d76f028.

Jew, Louise. "Stourbridge Mum Jayne Harris Reveals How She Became a Haunted Doll Investigator." Stourbridge News. September 4, 2015. https://www.stourbridgenews .co.uk/news/13646401.stourbridge-mum-jayne-harris -reveals-how-she-became-a-haunted-doll-investigator/.

Kershner, Jim. "Painting Goes Bump in the Night." The Spokesman-Review.com. October 31, 2002. https:// web.archive.org/web/20050120212242/http://www .spokesmanreview.com/news-story.asp?date=103102 &ID=s1244540.

Kettler, Dan. "The Janesville Baby." YouTube. 9 min., 34 sec., November 30, 2008. https://www.youtube.com/watch?v =lPxHLY1XAJo.

Kirkup, Rob. *How Haunted? Podcast.* how-haunted.com.

L., Michelle. "Fun Little Side Tour." Tripadvisor, June 18, 2016. https://www.tripadvisor.co.uk/ShowUserReviews -g34345-d130356-r383757091-Fort_East_Martello _Museum-Key_West_Florida_Keys_Florida.html.

Lawrence, Christopher. "Zak Bagans Conquered the Dyb-buk Box During His Quarantine." *Las Vegas Review-Journal.* June 5, 2020. https://www.reviewjournal.com /entertainment/tv/zak-bagans-conquered-the-dybbuk -box-during-his-quarantine-2045965/.

Lockett, Eleesha. "Understanding Automatonophobia: Fear of Human-Like Figures." Reviewed by Timothy J. Legg. Healthline. November 12, 2019. https://www.healthline .com/health/anxiety/automatonophobia.

Lodge, Sally. "Raggedy Ann Turns 100." Publishers Weekly. PWxyz. September 22, 2015. https://www.publishers weekly.com/pw/by-topic/childrens/childrens-book -news/article/68132-at-100-raggedy-ann-embodies -a-creative-family-legacy.html.

Lucia. "Encyclopaedia of the Impossible: Letta the Haunted Doll ('Letta Me Out')." The Ghost In My Machine. September 9, 2024. https://theghostinmymachine .com/2024/09/09/encyclopaedia-of-the-impossible -letta-the-haunted-doll-letta-me-out/.

Lucia. "Encyclopaedia of the Impossible: Pupa the Haunted Doll." The Ghost In My Machine. July 10, 2023. https://theghostinmymachine.com/2023/07/10/encyclopaedia-of-the-impossible-pupa-the-haunted-doll/.

"Mandy." Quesnel Museum & Archives. Accessed January 27, 2025. https://www.quesnelmuseum.ca/node/264.

"Meet One of Australia's Most Haunted Dolls in Warwick." The Courier Mail. March 1, 2018. https://www.couriermail.com.au/news/queensland/warwick/meet-one-of-australias-most-haunted-dolls-in-warwick/news-story/b787c3e75263b4f84ce03b19212ec45e.

Miller, Adam. "This Morning Viewers Genuinely Terrified By Haunted Doll as They Spot THIS—Did You?" Express. July 24, 2017. https://www.express.co.uk/showbiz/tv-radio/832361/This-Morning-viewers-terrified-haunted-doll-rocking-chair-Ruth-Langsford-Eamonn-Holmes-ITV/1000.

Miller, Maggie. "Paranormal Playthings: The World's Most Famous Haunted Dolls." Travel Channel. Accessed February 19, 2025. https://www.travelchannel.com/ghostober/articles/paranormal-playthings-the-worlds-most-famous-haunted-dolls.

Moss, Charles. "Finally, the Truth Behind the 'Haunted' Dybbuk Box Can Be Revealed." Inverse. July 8, 2021.

https://www.inverse.com/input/features/dybbuk
-box-dibbuk-kevin-mannis-zak-bagans-haunted
-hoax-revealed.

"Okiku: The Haunted Doll (Ep. 133)." Uncanny Japan. September 30, 2023. https://uncannyjapan.com/podcast
/okiku-the-haunted-doll/.

"'Possessed' China Doll Strikes Again! Mother Sells It for
£1,000 on eBay After It 'Scratched' Her Husband—Only
for New Owner to Claim His Father Has Now Been
Attacked Too." *Daily Mail*. August 4, 2017. https://www
.dailymail.co.uk/news/article-4760570/A-haunted-doll
-flogged-eBay-attacked-new-owner.html.

Quinata, Anthony. *Harold The Haunted Doll: The Terrifying,
True Story of the World's Most Sinister Doll*. Published by
the author, 2015.

Schuldt, Clay. "'World Has Always Been Crazy': Bizarre
History Enthralls Audience." *The Journal*. January 22,
2021. https://www.nujournal.com/news/local-news
/2021/01/22/world-has-always-been-crazy-bizarre
-history-enthralls-audience.

shawnfury. "Janesville, the Old Man & the Doll in the
Window." TVFURY. October 3, 2012. https://tvfury
.wordpress.com/2012/10/03/janesville-the-old-man
-the-doll-in-the-window/.

"The Story of the eBay Haunted Painting, from the Artist's Perspective." Stoneham Studios. Accessed February 19, 2025. https://stonehamstudios.com/haunted.

SublimeSloth. "Friend Disrespected Robert the Doll in Key West. Cursed Photo Result Followed. 100% Real." Reddit. Accessed March 4, 2025. https://www.reddit.com/r/Paranormal/comments/15cjb97/friend_disrespected_robert_the_doll_in_key_west/?rdt=33995.

Taylor-Blake, Bonnie. "Defrosting Frozen Charlotte: 21st-Century Misconceptions about a 19th-Century Doll." *So They Say* (blog). WordPress. July 6, 2019. https://btaylorblake.com/2019/07/06/defrosting-frozen-charlotte-21st-century-misconceptions-about-a-19th-century-doll/.

This Morning. "My Haunted Doll Attacked My Husband | This Morning." YouTube. 5 min., 44 sec. July 24, 2017, https://www.youtube.com/watch?v=f8nN-KG0UtM.

Vignes, Terri Lynn. "Haunted Doll." Accesed January 28, 2025. https://web.archive.org/web/20070410112535/http://www.hauntedamericatours.com:80/hauntedfurniture/haunteddoll/myhaunteddoll/.

"What Is a Shabti?" National Trust. Accessed March 4, 2025. https://www.nationaltrust.org.uk/discover/history/art-collections/shabti-faqs.

DOLL TRADEMARKS

Barbie is a registered trademark of Mattel, Inc.

Cabbage Patch Kids are a registered trademark of Original Appalachian Artworks, Inc.

Chatty Cathy is a registered trademark of Mattel, Inc.

Chucky is a registered trademark of Universal Studios.

Raggedy Ann is a registered trademark of Hasbro, Inc.

Shrinkin' Violette is a registered trademark of Mattel, Inc.

To Write to the Author

If you wish to contact the author or would like more information about this book, please write to the author in care of Llewellyn Worldwide Ltd. and we will forward your request. Both the author and the publisher appreciate hearing from you and learning of your enjoyment of this book and how it has helped you. Llewellyn Worldwide Ltd. cannot guarantee that every letter written to the author can be answered, but all will be forwarded. Please write to:

Fiona Dodwell
⁄ Llewellyn Worldwide
2143 Wooddale Drive
Woodbury, MN 55125-2989

Please enclose a self-addressed stamped envelope for reply,
or $1.00 to cover costs. If outside the U.S.A., enclose
an international postal reply coupon.

Many of Llewellyn's authors have websites with additional information and resources. For more information, please visit our website at http://www.llewellyn.com.